Role and Status of Women in Agricultural Development

NEELMA KUNWAR

AKANSHA PUBLISHING HOUSE
NEW DELHI

AKANSHA PUBLISHING HOUSE
4649-B/21, Ansari Road
Darya Ganj, New Delhi - 110 002
Email: ektabooks@yahoo.com
Ph. : 23263193 / 9811582579

Role and Status of Women in Agricultural Development

First Publisher 2006
ISBN 81-8370-061-6

[The responsibility for the facts stated, conclusions reached etc. is entirely that of the Authors. The publisher is not responsible for them, whatsoever.]

PRINTED IN INDIA

Published by M.P. Misra for Akansha Publishing House, New Delhi and Printed at Mehra Offset Press, Delhi.

Dedicated to
MY PARENTS

Preface

Most of the development literature till seventies failed to give equivitable importance to the participation of women in various economic activities. Consequently the formulation of developmental strategies in almost all the regions of world was base on near total ignorance of the nature and degree of women's work participation. The gradual deficiency in developmental strategies helped in shifting the focus in recent years to the studies of several social-economic aspects of women's productive contribution to the economy. In India, several macro-level studies have been conducted in the past to provide real insights about how and to what extent developmental forces have influenced the nature of women's involvement in several socio-economic activities. Hence, I have made a modest attempt to analyze, at micro level, role performance of rural women of Western Uttar Pradesh which determines to a great extent the success and failure of agriculture development at village level which inturn influence the rural economy.

For speedy development process, several technologies have been introduced in recent past. The ideology behind their introduction was that all the problems of human being would be solved by this appropriate application, the technology is appropriate for women if it reduces their drudgery, improves their skill and enhances their comfort but, after introduction of modern agricultural technologies, they were gradually displaced form work and their activities have been shrunked. For solving the plight of rural women, which technology would be appropriate has been identified in this study.

The encouragement and suggestion that I have received from my teachers, Professors V. Prasad and S.M. Dinger, friends and colleagues have helped to sustain my interest in this venture. Members of my family continues to be a source of inspiration for me.

I take this opportunity to acknowledge my debt of gratitude to the publisher M/s Akansha Publishing House, New Delhi for their painstaking efforts.

NEELMA KUNWAR

Acknowledgements

My debts are great and too many, especially like the debt of god, which I can nit even dare to knowledge, and who bestowed on me the courage to carry out this research work.

I feel great deal of pleasure to express my warm veneration and deep sense of gratitude to reverend Dr. H.P.S. Arya, Ex-Prof. and Head, Department of Livestock Extension, I.V.R.I., Izatnagar, Dr. B.P. Sinha, Ex-Head, Division of Agricultural Extension, R.B.S. College, Bichpuri, Agra for their talented and inspiring guidance and overcoming intricate problems throughout the investigation.

My profound obeisance are due to Dr. Vishnu Prasad, Ex-Professor (Agril. Economics) and Dr. S.M. Dingar, Associate Professor (Statistics), C.S. Azad University of Agriculture and Technology, Kanpur for not only suggesting the research problem but also took keen interest throughout the course of investigation. Had they not taken painstaking efforts and inspiring attitude, the research work would have not been accomplished.

I am highly indebted to Mr. B.N. Tiwari, I.A.S., Ex-Chief Secretary, Govt. of U.P. and Mr. Anis Ansari, I.A.S., Principal Secretary (Planning), Govt. of U.P. for sparing their valuable time and helped in providing materials required during the study.

I am also thankful to Dr. R.P. Singh, Ex-Director of Extension, N.D. University of Agriculture and Technology, Faizabad, and Dr. J.P. Singh, Ex-Head, Department of Agril. Extension, R.B.S. College Bichpuri, Agra for extending their valuable suggestions whenever required.

I also acknowledge Dr. R.N. Verma, Associate Professor (Agronomy) and Mr. A.K. Singhal, Associate Professor (Agril. Engg.), C.S. Azad University of Agriculture and Technology, Kanpur for their solemn co-operation and liberal contribution in the research work.

I am highly indebted to my brother-in-law Mr. S.B. Saxena, Ex-Minister, U.P. Govt.; my younger brother Soni, his wife Kanchan and niece Body Litasha for extending time-to-time encouragement in completion of this work.

I am also thankful to all my friends, colleagues and relatives who extended moral support to me during the entire period of study.

Lastly, I acknowledge all the selected respondents of the study area for their co-operatuon in collection of information during the personal interview with them.

Kanpur
30 May, 2006

NEELMA KUNWAR

Contents

List of Tables

CHAPTER 1

Introduction

In the history of human civilization, the advent of agriculture was the beginning of settled life. With the settlement of erstwhile nomadic people, the relationship of family, kinship and community crystalised, and women assumed special role in the family. They made significant contribution in settled agriculture. Thus, beginning of agriculture had a special significance in defining and determining the role and status of women throughout the world.

In all the communities of the world, women do not function merely as human incubators. They share the duties and responsibilities of maintaining their families on more than equal term with their men-folk but because of low visibility of their contributions; they are not regarded as equal partners in development process in spite of legal and constitutional equality.

In our society, where economic power rests with men, convention decreed that woman's place be in the home and that her husband's words are the law. Social customs and marriage-vows bound her to a life of drudgery of meek submission of house keeping and child bearing and child-care. Her household duties required between twelve to sixteen hours of work daily. She had very little time or opportunity for amusement, relaxation, or recreation – certainly none for a career of her own or for any hobbies or avocation worthy of mention. It is contended that she is borne for marriage and her interest in work or studies or her participation in social welfare will lead her to disturb her equilibrium in harmful ways.

Women are the cultural victims in our society, which provides superiority to men and institutionalizes deprivation to women. Had they been given the same opportunities as enjoyed by their men-folk, the progress and prosperity of the nation would have been manifold, but the traditional attitudes of both men and women and the values regarding rights and responsibilities confined women to the role of mothers and homemakers.

As the prosperity and growth of any nation depend on the status and development of its women because they are the foundation stone of the family in particular and society in general, the traditional attitudes which deprived women of opportunities outside their home have to be changed.

STATUS OF THE WOMEN

Status of any individual very much depends on the role or roles one performs since varying levels of values and prestige are associated with different roles.

In a traditional society where patriarchal family system prevails, the women are confined to the four-walls of the house. This limits their mental horizon and they are considered incompetent to make major decisions. They do not take part in the family decision-making process. Thus, they become dependent and remain agent rather than actors.

The status of women is governed by cultural values of the society. In case of Indian women, they are differentiated in real life according to caste, class religion, region, and so on. The cultural barriers are causing hindrance in raising status of women, particularly of rural women. Their status can only be raised if there is no *purdah* system imposed on them, no restriction on their physical movement, etc. hence, there is an urgent need for break down of cultural barriers through improvement in their education and economic emancipation (Prakash, 2000)1. No meaningful progress can be achieved without the active participation of women and the enhancement of their status. Greater attention is required to be paid on the promotion of their literacy, vocational training, providing market and credit facilities, and participation in the decision-making process.

ROLE OF WOMEN

Like other countries of the world, in India too, rural women actively participate in many agriculture and animal husbandry related activities, besides their usual role of child bearing and home keeping. Rural households are the basic productive units in India and women play a very significant and critical role in various agricultural operations – storage of grains, animal husbandry, and social forestry.

Women are traditionally known for their skills in the selection and storage of seeds, collection of fuel and fodder, livestock management, organic recycling, etc. Women, as compared to men, in small and marginal farm families in the villages carry a very heavy load of work both on the farm and in the house, with very limited access to and control over the resources necessary for farming or home keeping. Having an important role in agriculture, their nature and extent of involvement in it vary greatly from region to region, farming system, caste, classes, socio-economic status of families, etc.

According to 1991 census, women constituted 32 per cent of the labour force in the preparatory work before cultivation, 76 per cent for sowing seeds, 90 per cent for transplanting, 82 per cent in transporting the crops from fields, 100 per cent in traditional food processing and 69 per cent in dairying. Of the total women main workers, 38 per cent were women cultivators and 4.63 per cent engaged in livestock, fisheries, etc.

The type of work which women do depends on the social class to which they belong. Among the larger land owning households, they do no t do manual work in the fields whereas of small landholding families work on their own lands. Among the landless, there is work both in the field and in the house or compound of the employer. The dual burden of the lower class women emanates from the unequal power relations within patriarchal family.

It is frequently stated that women tend to withdraw from agriculture as the size of their land holding increases. Whenever the size of the family's land holdings increase, and the family becomes more prosperous, women are required to do many other works such as cooking foods for labourers during transplanting, harvesting and threshing seasons, supervising the work done and taking care of other things associated with the farms and house.

In identical situations, women are equal in efficiency and performance to make workers. In certain activities, they are even more efficient than their male counterparts. In case of paddy transplanting, they are 16 per cent more efficient than male workers are. The requirement of women labourers for paddy transplanting is only 118 man hours per hectare as against 137 man hours per hectare of male labourers for same work. The tasks, which they do not perform, are arduous and, hence, they are excluded from it.

APPROPRIATE TECHNOLOGIES FOR WOMEN

It is an increasing realization that for speedy development, the rural women need to be made aware of new agricultural and home technologies, which may raise their productivity, alleviate drudgery, and save energy and time. The task of upgrading traditional household activities and skills is a challenging one, as rural women" needs vary widely. They are mostly from lower-income families, illiterates, and the social stigma restricts their wholehearted adoption of new knowledge, skills, or innovations. Thus, what are required most urgently are low-cost improvements and innovations which will help in reducing fatigue and drudgery, conserve energy and utilise available resources efficiently. The technological development can help women only if it is used by them properly. It is felt that only a very small proportion of developed technologies has been adopted by the women.

The new technology introduction has no doubt helped the efficiently or effectiveness of work output and productivity both at home and farm. The mechanisation of operations has also helped in reduction of drudgery but these helped the economically better off farmers or to the male workers (Devnani, 1993)2. The irony is that whenever new technologies have been evolved for women specific jobs, the female workers are pushed out of their jobs and tasks have been taken by males. The resultant is that they are denied the chance of earning their livelihood and economic independence. For instance, when rice milling was introduced to remove the tedium of hand grinding and hand pounding of rice, men got the job and women pushed to other tedious tasks.

Women need to know the essential technologies in the thrust areas like seed production, raising of nurseries/plants, post-harvest technologies, storage of farm produce, etc. the post-harvest technologies as a multi-disciplinary applied science and engineering have been evolved for scientific conservation of agricultural produce by eliminating avoidable losses, and for making available more nutritive foods and high value of products from low grade raw materials by processing, fortification, packaging, transport and marketing. Apart from post-harvest technologies, lot of improved technologies has been evolved in the recent past, which not only can raise the crop productivity but also are effective in time saving energy, and cost, reducing drudgeries.

In the area of food processing, there are many new and existing technologies under way. Besides, the preservation of fruits and vegetables in the form of jams and pickles, new techniques of preserving vegetables through fermentation in earthen pot or polyethylene bags have been tried out. Solar dying of grains and preparation of a variety of breakfasts, cereals provide newer avenues for income generation of rural women.

As the farm women are burdened with a large number of households and other chores, the technologies introduces should be aimed at reducing the drudgery involved in these chores. They should be such that they save time in household activities so that they can undertake work on farm or outside with ease. The most difficult task which women face is fuel-wood collection and its use in a smoke-filled kitchen. The traditional '*chulha*', which the rural women ordinarily use, is highly inefficient and hazardous to their health. With constant exposure to smoke, they suffer from eye diseases, respiratory problems, and other ailments. The introduction of smokeless *chulhas*, biogas, and solar cookers has replaced traditional 'chulhas' in some parts of the country.

A lot of technologies have been generated and introduces for the benefit of women, but still there is an urgent need to disseminate them for strengthening women and thereby exploiting their hidden potentials.

WOMEN'S WORK PROFILE

The definition of women's work and its measurement by official agencies are questionable since their agricultural work is considered totally productive, animal husbandry productive and house-work totally non-productive work. Even though micro-studies have pointed to a much larger percentage of female population as main workers within families have, the numbers are certainly underestimated in official calculations.

Feminists have provided enough ethnographic data to question the earlier male-oriented definition of work. A distinction has been made by them between 'visible' work of men and 'invisible' work of women. Activities are instrumental in making women's work 'visible' and putting it on the agenda of development planners. Census of 1991 has made women's work such as agricultural activities and household production 'visible' but no serious attempt appears to have been made in estimating the value of house work in monetary terms.

The innumerable production activities carried out mainly by women with the household sector fare of critical importance for society's survival, growth, and development. In most of the societies, house work has emerged as privatised women's work and is, therefore, considered as non-productive 'unpaid' work because it is just family work which has no exchange value. They spend much of their time in 'unpaid' household activities, whether identified as economic productive or maintenance activities. These unpaid household activities are quite arduous, monotonous and isolating since it is performed and utilised within the household. Their 'unpaid' household activities provide a major contribution to the family, but their work in the production of goods and service in the family for its own consumption is inadequately measured and not considered in calculation of national income. Even when they are producing for the market, their work often does not computed in the market oriented concepts of income and employment, on account of being seasonal, intermittent casual and subsidiary nearly one-third of GNP. The failure to value work reduces them to virtual non-entities of development policies (Kulshrestha and Gupta, 2000).

Working women bear a double burden of doing 'unpaid' as well as 'paid' work. Patriarchal perception ignore their crucial role in the economy, relegating it to being 'supplementary', and they are considered as 'reproducers' and not 'producers'. In our society, people accept them to be inferior and submissive at home and at the work place. They are expected to be physically weak and docile, and are also expected to put the needs of family members above their own concerns.

The bondage between home and woman is more intense, and to run a home is a career in itself. If she chooses another career, she necessarily has to reconcile between the two roles, but under economic pressure which over riding the domestic responsibilities, she has to perform both 'paid' and 'unpaid' works. Despite cultural, regional, and temporal differences, she combines domestic work with wage work and the diminution of the farmer has not been substantial because of the later.

TIME UTILIZATION PATTERN

The number of hours spent by rural women in house and farm works depends upon the nature of the activity. The average work day for women is much longer than that of men, because there exists no clear demarcation line between 'productive' and 'unproductive' work in the case of women. Household works takes away a considerable proportion of the farm women's time, especially in fetching water and collecting fuel wood but during peak agricultural season the time spent on household work gets reduced. On an average, a farm woman worked for about 3 hours daily during peak agricultural season and find work for 6 to 7 days in the week. In animal husbandry tasks, during peak agricultural season, she devotes 2 hours daily. In household activities, during lean period, she devotes on an average 6.5 hours per day (Tripathi and Arya, 1988)4.

In low-income group rural families, women have a very heavy load of work both on the farm and in the home, with very limited access to and control over the resources necessary for farming or home making. On an average, they spend 28 per cent of their time in agricultural activities and 36 per cent in household activities whereas rural women of high-income group families devote on similar activities respectively 12.5 and 41.67 per cent of their time. Thus, the high-income group of rural women spends more time in household activities than their counterpart of low-income group.

WORK PARTICIPATION RATE (WPR)

The WPR of women continues to be less than that of men. In case of rural males, there has been a slight decline in WPR from 53.8 per cent in 1971 to 52.5 per cent in 1991. While it increased in case of women form 15.9 per cent to 27.2 per cent in the respective years. During 1981-91, 4 per cent increase was registered in women's work participation rate. The increase in women's employment should not be taken as a positive sign as this is a result of replacement of women for men at lower wages and worse work conditions.

WOMEN IN LABOUR FORCE

Economic growth and rising income per capita have a dramatic impact on the type of work households do, the income they receive, the way they manage their time and the sectors in which they work. Households also decide who will work and in which activities. As work is conventionally measured, men work more than women.

The labour force participation of women often changes in significant ways as development proceeds. Female participation rates tend to be higher when an economy is organised around family-based production in agriculture.

FARM SECTOR

Agricultural labour and farm cultivation is the main areas of economic activities for rural women. The NSS 27th round has shown that percentage contribution of women in farm sector is higher than men, where most of the key operations at farm are performed by them.

According to 1991 census, 22.73 per cent of total women population were workers, and among rural women workers 87 per cent were agricultural workers (India, 2001). About 38 per cent of the main women workers were cultivators and 49 per cent agricultural labourers. The proportion of women agricultural workers has been higher at 36.15 per cent as compared to male workers at 31.8 per cent. The increase in women's employment as wage workers is on account of migration of men to high-income jobs in cities. Sometimes, the migration is temporary for seasonal jobs.

The share of casual workers among total rural women workers went up between the years 1990 to 1994 from 41.0 to 45.3 per cent and the number of self employed women went down from 54.5 to 51.3 per cent, and that of regular workers from 4.5 to 3.4 per cent.

Animal husbandry and dairying are jobs mainly done by women and children among poorer peasant and agricultural workers families. Of the 100 million women engaged in dairying and animal husbandry works, 75 million engaged in dairying only. They not only milk animal but also control the rate of milk in the market.

NON-FARM SECTOR

According to 1991 census, about 13 per cent of total women main workers were engaged in non-farm sector. Only one in six working women engaged themselves in non-agricultural works such as construction activities, mining and quarry, trade and commerce, etc. almost all the women of low-income group families engaged themselves in non-agricultural works during slack agricultural season to supplement family income.

GENERAL PROBLEMS OF WOMEN WORKERS

Women's participation in labour force is necessary for society's development as well as for their survival. In terms of absolute numbers, their participation in work force has increased in organised and unorganised sectors. However, the majorities of women workers who are working in unorganised sector of economy face worst working conditions and are exploited by employers in terms of wages over work, etc. whatever has been done so far for their upliftment, and for giving them equal status with men have no significant effect on their status and even today they continue to face several problems.

WAGE DISCRIMINATION

In agricultural work, and also in construction, the work women do is invariably identified as light or unskilled and a lower wages are given. It is unfortunate that even when their output on a job is the same as that of men and their employment does not entail additional costs, they are paid less than men for similar work. Except in certain parts like Kerala, Punjab, Haryana, and Western U.P., the agricultural labourers do not receive the notified minimum wages and even in these parts, females do not get remuneration as per the notified minimum wages.

The wage discrimination between men's and women's job may be logical or justifiable if it is the result of the lower level of physical strength or responsibilities required in women's jobs but there is no justification for low payment to women for the same a comparable work.

NON-RECOGNITION OF WORK

Even today, as in the past, the household activities of women absorb a very large part of their time and energy. Indispensable but unpaid home-based activities persuade by women are not considered as economic activity and, therefore, not counted as employment, their work in the production of goods and services in the family for their own consumption is not considered in arriving at national income. The irony is that their talents and capacities remain unutilized as a human resource.

LESS BARGAINING POWER

Rural women workers are totally ignorant about whatever little legal protection are given to them. They are unaware of their rights and have to ensure implementation of the legislation. The result is that they do not get the benefits of collective bargaining as their counterparts in organized sector enjoy.

IMPACT OF MODERNISATION

Introduction of modern technology had led to women's displacement form work and lack of entitlement for income.

The technological development in agriculture has displaced them from agricultural activities to non-agricultural activities to a greater extent. In the absence of any substitute for economic activity, they are the worst sufferers. Even where technological innovations have been introduced in women-specific activities, those have been taken over by men simply because they lack skill and capital.

INCREASE IN UNPAID WORK BURDEN

The economic crises for the poor have led to an increase in the unpaid work burden of rural women. The implications of the Structural Adjustment Policies (SAP) have been typically negative, in terms of reduced real incomes and standard of living for most women, along with a greater burden of unpaid work. In fact, one very common gender specific result of such policies is the increase in the unpaid labour women.

DRUDGERY INVOLVED WORK

Drudgery is, generally, conceived as physical and mental strain, agony, monetary and hardship experienced by human beings. It affects the living and working conditions of men and women alike, but the plight of women in this regard is challenging as they continue to be constrained by illiteracy, malnutrition, and unemployment. Drudgery ridden tasks are, generally, assigned to women because of male dominated social order. All the works, irrespective of nature, equally involved large amount of physically and mentally, outside and inside their home, respectively.

On the basis of above expositions, it seems that rural women constitute so significant part of the working women population in our country that it necessitate a fuller understanding of their status and role not only as they now are but as they may be developed in the future. As no official statistics are available on the role and status of rural women of western Uttar Pradesh in agricultural, and also quite a few but sporadic and lop-sided studies on this aspect are available, much additional research work is needed for the study of their role and status in agricultural and non-agricultural works, and the problems they encounter in effectively discharging their responsibilities. The following objectives will be studied under the study-

1. To study the agro-climatic and socio-economic features of the study area with special reference to agricultural characteristics, occupational structure of working population and adoption of rural development programme.
2. To study the socio-economic profile of the sample households and examine the existing resource position of households under study.
3. To study the extent of knowledge, interest and adoption of modern agricultural and home technologies by farm women.
4. To examine the nature and degree of involvement of rural women of different socio-economic groups in farming systems and homestead activities, especially in terms of- (a) operations, (b) time spent and (c) period of involvement.
5. To examine the nature and level of employment of women in agricultural and non-agricultural sectors in the study area.
6. To identify the appropriate farm technologies which would provide the maximum advantages to rural women in terms of (a) enhancement of production efficiency, (b) increasing income, (c) reducing drudgery, and (d) increasing community participation.
7. To identify the socio-economic problems and suggest suitable policy measures for improving the status of rural women workers.

CHAPTER 2

Review of Literature

Arya (1964) observed that the younger male family depended more on female members for decision making than old family heads. Constancy of women decreased with the increase in the age of male family heads. However, the women continued to influence the decision regarding home management, irrespective of the age of male family heads.

Bhatia and Deshpande (1967) reported that the selected independent variables- caste, age, education, urban content and socio-economic status showed no definite relationship with the discontinuance or non-acceptance of the smokeless *chullha*. There was a non-significant relationship to the independent variables such as caste, age, education and socio-economic status.

Dhawan and Zohal (1967) reported that farm income could be increased through improved level of production techniques and planning resources use. Further, if the farmers were interested in the regular flow of income throughout the year, commercial dairy enterprises had the potentialities, but compared to the optimum production plan with only crop enterprises, some income had to be foregone. The plan yielded higher returns to the fixed farm resources as compared to the returns from the existing production plan of the cultivators. Finally, dairy enterprises, introduced at modern level, would also be pattern of resource use by any of more regular employment throughout the year with no adverse effect on land use efficiency.

Pauililo (1976) studied the extent to which rural women are integrated into agricultural production process and found that women of small farms and wives of share croppers contributed to production but received no remuneration, while of average and large farms, women also contributed but were usually paid and wives of wage earners rarely worked.

Acharya (1979) noticed that women's participation in labour force is a function of the total (dis)utility derived out of market work, leisure and home work. If the price of market work goes up, with other things given constant, the labour force participation rises. However, if the household income (meaning husband's income) rises then the relative disutility of work increases, and women tend to withdraw from the labour force. These are the inducing and non-inducing factors, which determine the participation or withdrawal of women from the labour force. The discontinuties in employment along with break in services for bearing and rearing children is the reason why women are unable to acquire skills otherwise acquired by men. This leads to gender specific wage differentials. Wage differentials are also attributed to the voluntary foresight of women in choosing jobs requiring lesser skills as they envisage service breaks and shorter life time work for themselves. Of course, the profit maximizing instinct of the employers coincides with the women employees' thought and they do not employ women in jobs requiring very high sophistication.

Bala and Roy (1979) postulated that personal and social characteristics of trained and untrained farm women did not differ much in respect of age, education, family type, caste belongingness and income level. It was inferred that on the whole trained had some association with knowledge of the selected practices. The study further revealed that age was positively correlated and education was negatively correlated with the use of knowledge of food preparation, however, their relationships were not significant. Social participation was also positively and significantly correlated with the knowledge on labour saving devices.

Deepali (1979) said that the participation of rural women in agricultural operations varied on the basis of caste, age, education and extension contact.

Sampath (1979) reported that the difference between the small farmers and the large farmers in terms of the level of economic efficiency achieved was insignificant. Economic inefficiency of the small farmers was 35.27 per cent in comparison to 37.83 per cent of the large farmers.

Anandlakshmy and Kelkar (1980) revealed that during the harvesting seasons. Utilization of women labour is maximum. Carrying bundles of harvested crop to the spot where threshing would be done is a heavy task performed mostly by women. Each bundle is carried as a head load by women, mostly bare footed, walking over the sharp shrubs of the harvested fields. Men rarely participated in this task.

Chopra (1980) observed a negative and significant correlation between gain in knowledge and age of the respondent and also the retention of gained knowledge and age of the respondent. He also found that social participation and gain in knowledge were positively correlated whereas size of holding had no significant relationship with gain in knowledge of cattle diseases.

Jain (1980) quoted that women in Gujarat are, generally, associated with animal husbandry activities which are performed at home viz., cattle feeding, milking, fodder preparation and cleaning of shed. While the men are, generally, engaged in tasks which are performed outside the home, viz., procurement/ collection of cattle feed and fodder, pasture-grazing and offering water to animals.

Punia (1980) reported that agriculture is getting rapidly modernised in two ways in our country, firstly, in mechanisation with accelerated installation of tubewells, pumpsets, diesel engines and, secondly, by the improved agriculture technologies like high yielding variety (HYV) seeds, fertilisers, insecticides and pesticides.

Ruth (1980) stated that the farm work does not confine itself only to crop production and so any attempt to work out the dimensions of female worker employment by considering time spent in crop production alone would lead to unrealistic estimates of the problem. In order to find out the nature, pattern and dimensions of female workers' employment in a rural agrarian economy along with crop production, female labour days spent in other productive activities (i.e. non-crop work like grass cutting, cleaning the fields for the next crop, tending of cattle, labour days, hired and/or exchanged out, time spent for wage work, business, services and household industries) as well as time spent in necessary activities (i.e. household activities like cooking, rearing of children, washing utensils, fetching water, collection of wild vegetables, service of elders , days wasted in sickness and other family and social affairs) were also taken into consideration for analysing the pattern of female workers employment during the full agricultural year. All the above mentioned productive and necessary activities were taken into consideration.

Sinha (1980) opined that technological development in agriculture has resulted in intensive cultivation, occupational diversification, profit to the landed gentry and improvement in the level of living of the landlord class women. Though, there has not been any significant change either in the wage rates or in the living standard of peasantry and poor peasantry women, there has been marked change in the level of their social consciousness like family planning awareness and education.

The technological development in agriculture has displaced women from agriculture activities to in greater degree and have replaced them in non-agricultural activities.

Tinker (1980) expressed that women are the primary user of household energy and much of the energy is needed for subsistence activities. Interventions to change use of fuel at the village level must take into account the roles of women and the total time spent for carrying out their daily responsibilities.

Dhesai et al. (1981) found that food items cooked in the solar cooker were appreciably good and were acceptable for its appearance, shape, colour texture, flavour and doneness. However, the average scores obtained from organoleptic test for the products cooked in solar cooker were not much different from the scores of the product cooked on gas.

Jain (1981) studied the attributes of improved home practices as perceived by farm women and concluded that farm women perceived use of pressure cooker as profitable.

Jhansi Rani (1981) pointed out education was negatively correlated with type and extent of participation in farm tasks, but positively correlated with participation in decisions relating to expenditure pattern.

Kaur (1981) revealed in her findings that the maximum participation by farm women was in the activities like picking the pods and unsheathing the maize cobs. Middle-aged farm women as compared to young and old, daughter-in-law as compared to mother-in-law and daughters participated more in these activities. In case of farm activities performed at home, the most frequently participated activities were related to grain storage and in case of animals, participation in keeping accounts was the lowest, daughter-in-law participated maximum in all the activities performed at home except for taking care of equipment where mother-in-law participated maximum. She also observed that a majority of Muslim and lower caste Hindu women were involved in marketing of produce, whereas upper caste Hindus rarely participated in it. Participation in farm as well as home related physical activities was more for daughter-in-law as compared to mother-in-law and daughter of the households.

Dixon (1982) observed that ploughing and irrigation was main tasks, sowing may be restricted to men or women or shared, weeding and transplanting are women's tasks, harvesting is frequently shared and most of the post-harvest operations (threshing, winnowing, drying, husking, cleaning and storing) are performed by women.

Mahajan and Singh (1982) observed that education of homemaker, her income and membership of village organization are associated with the adoption of home making practices whereas socio-economic status and size of holding are not associated with their adoption.

Singh (1982) reported that education, awareness, knowledge, socio-economic status, extension contact, mass-media exposure and situational resources have positive and significant correlations with the adoption of dairy husbandry practices, whereas age, caste and principle knowledge have no significant correlation with the same.

Yadav (1982) observed that farm women in higher socio-economic status did not enjoy as much of involvement in decision-making process regarding farm operations as those of middle or lower socio-economic status families.

Bajwa (1983) observed that in farm owning families, majority of the respondents (60%) participated always in making poultry shed and 70 per cent in hatching and majority of them participated sometime in all other activities and in non-farm owning families majority i.e. 100 per cent participated always in hatching and majority of respondents participated sometime in all other activities. On the whole, the women from farm owning families participated more in sowing (0.66), storage (0.01) and miscellaneous activities (0.66), in all this case 1st, 2nd ranks were in case of threshing and operations during crop production, whereas women from non-farm owning families participated more in operations during crop production (0.23), harvesting (0.99), threshing (0.5) than women from farm owning families. Here , 1st, 2nd rank were in case of harvesting and sowing and 5th and 6th were in case of miscellaneous activities and operations during crop production, respectively.

Mazumdar (9183) found that as farm size increases, the hours spent on agricultural activities decrease, while the hours spent on non-agricultural activities increase. However, in general, the hours spent on agricultural activities stood at about one-third of the hours spent on non-agricultural activities.

Nagbrahman and Sambrani (1983) observed that substantial portion of women's working time and energy is devoted to such task as collecting fuel and water, cooking and looking after children. Among the poorer households, difficulties in collecting fire wood and fuel are increasing. People seem to be caught between a process of immunization caused by increasing pressure on scarce resources (and their poor command of the resources to begin with) on the one hand, and the process of development which has led to valuable alternative uses for resources which up-till now have been considered as waste (*and available to them free of cost) on the other. The increasing drudgery of rural women is seen to be an inseparable part of the overall depending poverty in the rural areas.

Saikia (1983) had worked out that work participation rates of females were 58.37 per cent in marginal farms, 57.7 per cent in small farms and 53.91 per cent in medium farms. Agriculture is the most important sector promoting employment to 97.54 per cent of the female workers both in primary and secondary occupations. Out of the total female workers engaged in farm activities, 84.38 per cent worked full time and only 15.62 per cent were engaged as part time workers.

Saini (1983) observed that female member of land-owning families spent relatively more time in kitchen as compared to those of non-land owning families.

Singh (1983) reported that participation of women was the highest in respect of seed storage (100%), followed by marketing of produce (94%). It was the least in respect of plant protection measures (10.5%), followed by application of manures and fertilizers (25.4%).

Sinha (1983) revealed that the women in higher income and education groups have favourable attitude towards education of women.

Jamal and Singh (9184) noticed that education was significantly and positively associated with the knowledge about nutritive value of green leafy vegetables, methods of cooking vegetables, use of smokeless *chullah* and use of germinated fermented and mixed food. It was further found that simplicity and complexity were significantly and positively associated with the knowledge about use of smokeless chullah, methods of food preservation and use of germinated, fermented and mixed food. Adoption was significantly associated with cultural compatibility among both small and marginal farm women.

Sreedevi (1984) reported that women from agriculturally progressive village spent on an average 8.2 hours per day compared to 7.6 hours per day by women from progressive village.

Duggal (1985) revealed that the time saved in preparing food on smokeless chullah over traditional chullah was about 43 to 46 per cent, the fuel saved was about 31 to 35 per cent while the money saved was about 10 to 25 per cent.

Mc Aulley (1985) pointed out that in most countries, agricultural work and agricultural organisation are much more intimately involved with culture than is true of metal fabricating. Agriculture, virtually in all countries, is subject to seasonal variations in its demand for labour. In Soviet climatic conditions, these variations are likely to be particularly acute, although, here, the size of the USSR and the range of climatic zones in which it is situated will introduce considerable regional differences. Since some activities are more dependent upon the weather than others, sexual specialisation may well result in differences in the monthly-by-month employment profiles of men and women. It may also contribute to the lower involvement of women in paid employment.

The division between work and home is less clear cut in agriculture than in most other areas of employment. It is sometimes possible for women to perform agricultural and domestic functions simultaneously. As a result, analysis of time budget materials for the light that they cast on women's double burden and the contribution that it makes to occupational segregation should properly be undertaken separately for the agricultural and non-agricultural labour forces.

Panghal and Ram (1985) pointed out that women labour was more efficient than men labour in respect of transplanting of paddy (16 % more), weeding in paddy and wheat (7 to 8 % more), picking of cotton (37 % more) and picking of jowar (25 % more).

Saxena and Bhatnagar (1985) suggested that participation of women in farm activities was more or less same for tribal as well as non-tribal farm women in Rajasthan. On an average, they use to devote 8.25 hours per day in agricultural activities.

Srivastava (1985) stated that women, irrespective of land status of the family, provide 14 to 18 hours of productive physical labour in different chores. The energy spent by them in performing these tasks is more than it is physically feasible for them to spend particularly in a below subsistence level of living. This draws our attention to the plight and drudgery of rural women.

Acharya (1986) has substantiated sufficiently with data that proposition like diffusion effects of new technology in agriculture is not sex-neutral. Introduction of modern technology had led to women's displacement from work and lack of entitlement for income. However, differential impact of the above changes on men and women needs a joint analysis of caste, class and gender.

Dak et al. (1986) observed that majority of farm women in Haryana played monopolising or dominant role in 8 out of 17 agricultural tasks. Three of them are tending cattle, collecting fodder and selling livestock products.

Gandhi et al. (1986) noted that besides taking care of almost all the household work, women also participate in most of the animal related activities. Collection and storage of manure, feeding cattle, looking after the milch cattle and poultry keeping were entirely the jobs of farm women in Haryana. They also observed that cooking, fetching water, washing (clothes and utensils), house maintenance and child care were major concerns of almost all families in all the selected districts (94.5%). These accounted for about 81/4 hours per day. Care of animals consumed on an average about 3 hours per day. About 41/4 hours per day were spent on leisure time activities. The remaining time was spent mostly on sleeping.

Kaur (1986) observed that improved agriculture technology accompanied by full mechanisation has negatively affected the women from lower castes, lower income groups who were either landless or had small land holding by reducing the demand for employment in peak season. Whenever, employment opportunities for all works are in short supply, women are most likely to be affected and, thus, suffer the adverse consequences.

Maurya (1986) observed that, in Indian society, women's place has been primarily confined to the home and their role is limited to procreation, rearing of children and catering for the needs of men folk by way of creature comforts. Usually, the women in developing countries like India perform multiple duties by combining all types of household work including child care with such other jobs as farming, animal husbandry, work in household industry, etc. depending upon the opportunities affected by the complex socio-economic and organisational structure of the life. The total work force may be considered as being made up of main workers plus marginal workers. If the participation rates for main workers and marginal workers are combined together, a significant increase in the participation rate in India is reported in the case of females but not in the case of males.

Bhati and Singh (1987) found that women's labour accounts for 61 per cent of total work that their participation ion animal husbandry is greater than in crop production, and that there is some trend toward sexual division of labour. Bhatty (1987) observed in his study that in 25 per cent of the sample households whose annual income did not exceed Rs. 1500, women's contribution to income was 77 per cent to 95 per cent. Nearly all households, with slight differences depending on family size, felt that they would not be in a position to maintain their existing standard of living without the income from *beedi* making, 77 per cent thought that they had better treatment in the household since they had been earning and 72 per cent thought that their views on spending decisions had required greater weight. The women experiencing this improvement in status increased with household size and income and, therefore, increased also with their own contribution. There was also evidence of a change in attitude towards women's working.

Kaur (1987) revealed that a very high percentage of women played role in the decisions regarding payment of dowry, food given to expectant and nursing mothers and storage of farm produce. However, they were not involved in decisions regarding education of children, taking loans for consumptive expenditures, expenditure pattern of family and farm related activities except storage and sale and purchase of animals.

Laxmi Devi (1987) stated that the low income category of rural women performed more work in farm activities while the high income category performed more work in home activities. Rural women in Andhra Pradesh spent on an average

40.4 and 15.8 per cent, respectively in home and farm related activities.

Lepha (1987) opined that average daily hours livestock production activities were about 7.2 hours per day.

Satapathy (1987) evaluated that participation of farm women in Orissa, especially in respect of small holdings, was quite substantial in respect of all important animal related activities.

Anandalakshmy and Sawhney (1988) observed that modernisation process in the agricultural sector including the introduction of HYV, quality seeds, fertilizers, pesticides and modern implements has pushed the women to less skilled jobs and as support agents rather than major handlers of equipments.

Modernisation did not change the pattern of employment for women, but affected the level of employment. Suitable technologies for rural women were lacking for transfer to rural masses. Even the women have been, generally, deprived of the beneficiary training component of the developmental as well as the poverty alleviation programmes under IRDP and DWCRA. They also reported that women play a prominent role in crop cultivation and post-harvest operations. All women in rural areas, irrespective of their age, size of their family, size of land holding, caste and community, perform major agricultural tasks. Women of landless labour families are the poorest, bearing a heavy burden of work in cultivation and performing even the task of land preparation, along with all other tasks.

Devdas et al. (1988) opined that the major cause for the contribution of women in agriculture is less significant due to dual role of farm women on the farm and in the home leading to drudgeries resulting out of inappropriate and cumbersome work methods and practices related to household chores of food preparation, fuel collection, water fetching, resource management and child rearing with regard to dissemination of agricultural technologies, sex bias is often seem reflecting in farmers having access to technologies.

Dubey (1988) noted that women also graze the animals on distant lands, collect fodder, wash the cattle, clean the sheds, feed the animals, milk them and take the milk for sale.

Ghosh and Adhikary (1988) have observed that regarding preference of the village women for different professions, dairy is the most preferred enterprise followed by agriculture, business and service. It is evident that low level of education and experience of village women are responsible for their present situation.

Hira Nand et al. (1988) explained that 62 per cent farm women devoted more than 8 hours per day for farm work during the peak period and 76 per cent of them devoted 4 to 6 hours per day during the slack season in Shimla. However, on plains, majority of women spent 6 to 8 hours per day in peak season and 2 to 4 hours per day during slack season in Bhojpur district of Bihar.

Kalaimathi (1988) observed that women participate in all the agricultural operations in the same way as general agricultural labourers, women agricultural labourers are divided into female cultivators, female agricultural labourers and other workers further subdivided into permanent labours and casual labours. The condition of women in the agricultural sector has remained the same over a long period. In the past, they were either labourers or assisted their husbands in some agricultural operations.

Kashyap (1988) studied that the mean time (irrespective of season) spent in household chores varied significantly from 7 hours 35 minutes by women of marginal to 9 hours 38 minutes by women from large land holdings in Haryana. Such differences from peak (7 hours 7 minutes) season were found to be significant. The study revealed that women from large land holdings spent more than 9 hours per day in these activities during both the seasons.

Kaur and Sharma (1988) observed that the new technology made no impact on the employment of women in the backward region of the backward district. In the advanced region of the developed district 47.4 per cent of the women worked for fewer days and only 15.1 per cent for more days.

All the women who got more employment were from the scheduled castes. Among those who were employed for fewer days, mechanization reduced the work-load of 10 per cent of the upper castes and 34 per cent of the intermediate class, while it reduced the employment of 19.4 per cent of lower castes and 13.6 per cent of the scheduled castes. All women in the higher income group had voluntarily withdrawn from labour force.

Women who got more employment were all agricultural labourers, whether they are landless or have small holdings, caste, nature of farm work, income, size of holding and intensity of mechanization in that order were associated with the number of days of employment.

Krishnamurthy and Kulkarni (1988) stated that considering the responsibilities of women in agricultural and home maintenance, and also their physical limitations, the agricultural technologists have to develop appropriate technologies to ensure gainful utilisation of the services of women. There is need to develop better technologies for agricultural operations as transplanting, weeding, harvesting and cleaning of crop products to reduce the physical burden and drudgery for the women. The operations like cleaning of cattle byre, collection of refuse, compost, biogas production in which the women are actively involved need to be more skill rather than labour oriented.

Kulkarni et al. (1988) found that among various operations like sowing, inter-culture and harvesting required more female labour than male labour. Further, they also observed that women from small farmers and landless agriculture labour family are mostly engaged in agricultural work while women from farmers having large holdings are engaged in domestic work.

Kunwar and Guleria (1988) in a study to examine the socio-economic pattern of farm families role and utilization of female labour in various farm operations, conducted in block Bhawarna of district Kangra during the agricultural year 1987-88, have observed that the number of female workers per farm per hectare were the highest in case of scheduled castes. The illiteracy among scheduled castes was 5.7 per cent as against 40 per cent in upper castes. The women are engaged in doing all farm operations except ploughing. Their participation in agricultural operations was higher than man. Weeding and transplanting are usually done by females. Milking is, exclusively, a feminine operation. The role of women in scheduled castes and backward castes is more important because they are also doing the farm operations on the farms of other castes over and above attending to their homes. It may be concluded that the role of women of these two categories is significant in enhancing the farm income and, thereby, improving the status of the family to a great extent.

Manick and Manimegali (1988) noticed that smokeless chulha is a simple device which can be made by local materials. It saves time 43 to 46 per cent, fuel by 31 to 33 per cent and cost of fuel by 25 per cent. Another device is the biogas plants. This saves the cooking time by one hour per day. This can also be operated with local resources. Both these will enhance the fuel efficiency, reduce drudgery and eliminate environmental pollution. Evapocooling chamber, a simple device to preserve the fruits and vegetables, extends the storage life of vegetables and reduces the weight loss in storage. Use of these appropriate technologies will save the cooking and marketing time of the rural women. They can use this time for productive employment by which their family income and nutritional status could be enhanced.

Maratha (1988) pointed out that in all regions except the rainfed paddy predominate region women as family farm labour perform in all agricultural operations. However, ploughing is dome exclusively by men whereas harvesting is carried by both men and women. Certain operations as winnowing, drying , storage and husking/milling in all regions are women's domain and transplanting is exclusively performed by women.

Pandey et al. (1988) found that the percentage of women to total family members employed on the farm decreased with the size of holding but large farms had relatively higher employment of female labour than small and medium farms. The major crops absorbing female labour were cotton, paddy, wheat and *rabi* fodder, and the major operations were weeding and hoeing, harvesting/picking, threshing and winnowing. Rural women worked between 9 and 14 hours a day and, in general, had only a supportive role in agricultural decisions. The size of operational holding and ratio of crops to total cropped area were positively and significantly related to the employment of rural women.

Tripathi and Arya (1988) studied that farm women devoted maximum time of her working hours in household activities (food preparation, cleaning and child care). Under this, food preparation took the maximum working hours of farm woman, i.e. 3 hours 45 minutes every day.

Vijaya and Singh (1988) observed that farm women are facing various problems mainly due to socio-economic hurdles and as such the comparative dependency on men is ,more in rural areas (economic participation is conspicuously low).

Nataraju and Lovely (1989) studied that women participated in a very large and considerable extend in 11 out of 17 family operations. Except ploughing operations, they have participated in all other operations to a large extent such as sowing/ transplanting (86%), weeding (84%), storage of grains (78%), land p reparation (72%), cleaning seeds for sowing (70%), gap filling (68%), manure and fertilizer application (68%), harvesting (64%), threshing and winnowing (62%), and rat control practices (58%).

Varma (1989) explained that the operations viz., pesticide dusting, spade work during field irrigation, ploughing, sowing, manure and fertilizer application, uprooting of seedlings and marketing of grains were exclusively performed by men. Transplanting and storage of grains were found to be exclusively domain of women in Haryana. The other farm operations like weeding, harvesting, carrying load on head, threshing and winnowing were jointly, but predominantly, performed by women.

The average work load of men and women of low socio-economic stratum was higher than those of high and medium socio-economic strata respondents in farm operations.

Verma (1989) in her study revealed that the total amount of drudgery in carrying out agronomic operations of paddy and wheat cultivation, shouldered by women, was found to be significantly higher than that shouldered by men. They seem to be in direct proportion of the time spent in performing various tasks by men as well as women. The amount of drudgery per man day of work shouldered by women was found to be significantly higher than that shouldered by men in case of wheat cultivation, but it was in the reverse order in case of rice cultivation.

Chakraborty (1990) observed that significant increase in agriculture production has been achieved in India through many avenues like use of better seeds, enrichment of soil by fertilizers and fair irrigation systems. But comparatively less attention has, however, been laid towards the improvement and modernization of agricultural tools. Considerable increase in agricultural production can be achieved by better tools having improved mechanical properties and wear resistance.

Modern scientific method for a productive agriculture is, thus, a natural issue in all developing countries. Considerable increase in agriculture production can be achieved by better tools and implements. Better tools increase the production capacity of men and animals and also provide ease and comfort in operations.

Jesani (1990) reported that agricultural tasks like transplanting, weeding and threshing are done by women but ploughing is dome by men only, showing division of labour within occupations is highly sex biased.

Kumar (1990) stated that agricultural mechanization has made a radical improvement in the production and productivity of Indian agriculture. The increase in agricultural production due to mechanization is quite wide spread in the plains, but the hilly areas have not realized the effect of mechanization due to variations in topography and different climatic and socio-economic constraints. Almost, all the agricultural operations (except ploughing) are carried out by the women alone or sometimes along with their male counterparts. Most agricultural operations in hills are dome manually except ploughing and puddling which are done by bullocks.

The use of efficient agricultural tools and implements plays an important role to increase agricultural production to feed the ever growing population, reduces the burden and drudgery of farm workers, and to increase the output per worker very significantly.

Using modern implements and tools, several field operations could be done quickly. More efficient and durable tillage tools and implements give the desired effect on the soil by requiring less energy per unit land area.

Pradhan (1990) stated that the identification, creation and promotion of appropriate agricultural technologies suitable for farm women like making of paper sacks (farm jute and mesta, cotton stalk, etc.) for packing tea leaves, etc. Preparation of vinegar from pineapple, technology for storing of vegetables under water, packaging systems, fish farming and molluscs farming etc. should be pursued. If women would have been trained for these jobs future prospect of agricultural sector would be brighter.

Savitri and Geeta (1990) emphasised that for the enthusiastic young generation of girls and women, tireless efforts are to be made for the better place of women in the society. India's future depends much on whether the Indian women have the wisdom and dissemination to distinguish between what to respect and what tot reject.

Sethi (1990) has classified the different household activities into three categories: those that have to be performed daily such as cooking and cleaning, those that have to be performed at least once a week such as washing and making *uplas* (cow dung cakes), and those that need to be performed occasionally such as weaving and stitching of cloths and repairing the 'chulhas'. It can be said that cooking of food and cleaning of utensils are exclusively done by females.

Shatrugna (1990) observed that the most over worked women are from the middle-peasant households, i.e., households with some land, cattle and other animals and that the women experience drudgery to a great extent as each of their seasonal tasks as winnowing, drying, preserving grains, grinding spices, etc. take chunk of her time in addition to mending clothes and caring sick and elderly family members.

Tripathi and Soudamini Das (1990) stated that a high proportion of working women in India are employed in the unorganized sector mainly in agriculture, livestock, forestry, the percentage being 79 as per 1981 census. Working women are manifested in agricultural activities like land preparation, seed grading, sowing, dibbling, planting, irrigating, threshing, winnowing, storing crops, feeding cattle, looking after milch animal and poultry, etc. The nature of works in agriculture which the women labourers perform exposes them to particular health hazards. Those unorganised has broad dimension like agriculture, animal husbandry, fisheries, home based industries like handicrafts, handlooms, coir industry, *agarbati* industry, *bidi* industry, sericulture, construction industry and the like.

In recent years, adequate attention has been focussed for the development of informal sector, which employs greater percentage of women labour. In the wake of rapid industrialisation and mechanisation, women experience acute unemployment consequent upon the delay of traditional crafts and handloom sector. They are unable to face the new challenge and participate in the advanced modern industrialized sector due to lack of skill and technology which is obstructed by family obligations and conservative attitude of the people.

Vashney (1990) found that tat present women are largely employed in the unorganised sector which turns them at comparatively low wage and poor facilities. The employment pattern as envisaged in our economy is a reflection of the type of training facilities available for women in India.

In India, even after 40 years of planned development, man power imbalances in certain (specially among young women) do persist although they are not desirable from the point of view of either the individual or the society or the nation. In order to remove these imbalances, adjustment to man power resources available in the country at different levels is very necessary, man power planning viz-a-viz educational planning can to a great extent help in reducing these imbalances.

Varma and Sinha (1990) stated that drudgery is, generally, conceived as physical and mental strain, agony, monotony and hardship experienced by human beings. While all of these result in decline in living and working conditions affecting men and women alike, the plight of the women in this regard is alarming as they continue to be constrained by illiteracy, malnutrition and unemployment. The findings of the study suggest that a very serious implication to a technological solution, if innovated, is to emancipate women from the drudgery they undertake in farm operations/tasks. On the face value of the problem, one can easily suggest that if suitable tools and techniques are invented to raise efficiency and reduce time and energy consumption in the tasks being predominantly performed by women, their work load and drudgery shall be reduced. The primary tasks, therefore, is to provide education to men and women both to explode the myth of the value that women are '*abala*' less powerful and have lower ability to acquire skills. An effort to innovate suitable technology for women and education to both men and women have to go hand in hand, otherwise the cherished goal of emancipating women of their drudgery in agriculture will remain unachieved.

Bihari (1991) observed that, in the Indian content, dispersal of industries for providing higher levels of income to the rural population is presently very important. The technological choice must be directed to this end. The task is not easy by the goal is worth pursuing. The decision for selecting one mode of production from the various available alternatives, rather it would involve adopting the different stages of production to the ecological and sociological conditions of the society. The need for this king of approach is immense in rural environment, but to make it effective, it will require a reformulation of our employment generating programmes, provision of common service facilities, and creation of infrastructure in accordance with agro-ecological potential and socio-economic needs of each area.

Jain (1991) evaluated that total drudgery and per man day drudgery taken up by women in animal husbandry operations were more than those taken up by men in Hisar district, but it was in reverse order in case of Kurukshetra district of Haryana where men perform more drudgery-prone activities than women in animal husbandry practices. He reported that in majority of cases, decisions were taken jointly by husband and wife in Hisar district but in kurukshetra district, majority of the decisions were taken alone by husbands.

Rajamal et al. (1991) revealed that 92 per cent women were involved in sowing, seeding and winnowing. Between 83 and 89 per cent women carried out transplanting, application of fertilizers, harvesting and threshing.

Sudharani and Raju (1991) said that women play a significant role in Indian agriculture. According to 1981 census, compared with 63 per cent of men, 79 per cent of female working population was actively engaged in agriculture. Almost 50 per cent of the rural female workers were working as agricultural labourers and 37 per cent as cultivators. Women as agricultural labourers participate in several activities such as seeding, transplanting, weeding, fertilizer application, plant protection, thinning, harvesting, processing, selling, winnowing, storing, looking after animals, kitchen gardening, etc. Several of these operations are exclusively carried out by women only. Thus, by participating in above agricultural activities, they directly or indirectly influence the course of agriculture.

Indravati et al. (1992) stated that raising the operational and managerial efficiency of women at home and farm, the drudgery related with home and farm activities must be minimized. The extent of drudgery involved in various household activities revealed that cooking was identified as the most drudgerious activity (Ist rank) by the expert. Cooking was carried out thrice a day and is a definite time task. Their kitchens were poorly organised devices.

Dahiya and Gupta (1993) opined that women perform dominantly the household activities like food preparation, washing of clothes while husbands were more willing to cooperate in child care and tasks which are not strictly traditionally female oriented in Haryana.

Dixon (1993) have observed that the most government and private welfare programmes aimed at raising the level of living of rural women and their families have concentrated on encouraging greater productivity in the home through training in child care and nutrition, cooking vegetable and poultry raising, sewing, and other activities coming under the general fabric of home economies. If they have addressed the issue of income-earning activities for women at all, they have encouraged cottage industries such as weaving, basket making, or embroidery with the products being marketed through intermediaries, local shops or co-operatives. They also stated that the rationale for locating income generating employment in rural areas is simple. The vast majority of the South Asian population is rural. Rural inhabitants experience more extreme poverty than do urban residents, in part because of the frequently high levels of both seasonal and permanent under and unemployment in the agricultural sector.

The decentralization of industrial development creates a diffusion effect by dispersing the sources of economic and social change throughout the country rather than concentrating them in urban centres.

The regions or among socio-economic or ethnic groups in which women currently play an important role in agriculture in the Himalayan regions, for example, or among the tribes and lower castes of India the best strategy may well be to integrate women more fully into the agricultural process.

Grover and Grover (1993) observed that the participation of women is essential for the well being of rural families and children. About 47 per cent of rural women are classified as agricultural labourers and 34 per cent as cultivators. The corresponding percentages for men are 20 and 44. This indicates that rural women have an inadequate control. Over the means of production and area highly dependent on recruitment of labour force. In their study, the authors found that full mechanization has reduced the demand even of casual labour, affecting women most.

Kaur and Mahajan (1993) reported that farm women were performing all the activities related to agriculture from pre-sowing to storage of grains and also activities like dairying.

Sen (1993) observed that resultant scenario of women wage earners in agriculture is that they suffer major disadvantages relative to men in their search for employment opportunities, lower real wages and greater uncertainty and irregularity of employment.

In order to improve upon the hapless condition of these women, they have to be provided with alternate and more productive employment opportunities. To improve the position of women work force, it is necessary to improve their production potential by treating them as important actors, not as dependent member of family.

Economic incentives, thus provided, will free the women from the shackles of inside/outside dichotomy. Increased economic productivity will be able to influence their status and image in the family as well as the wider societal level. The ability of the women to contribute more in the family income will provide them with a greater bargaining power.

Shanmugasundaram (1993) said that the bondage between home and women is more intense than that between men and home and this relationship is fundamental to any analysis of women's role in the economic field. To run the home is a career. She necessarily has to reconcile between tow roles. Her additional role of a worker throws many a challenge along with her primary challenges of the households.

Recently developments such as large number of women seeking work, and staying in jobs for longer periods have made an impact on labour theories. Women employment differs from that of men and is characterised by discontinuities due to marriage, child bearing, and post natal demands on her time at home.

Agarwal (1994) observed that one of the most important changes in the past 15 years has been the increase in the number of women who have achieved professional success, and who, at the same time, have borne children. The increase has been remarkable but the number is still small as only 14 per cent of women in India are in full time employment. The general employment situation as for as women are concerned is far from satisfactory. These women are an exception.

Baskara Rao (1995) observed that longer duration of work and time bound work schedules that ate generally characteristics of modern irrigated farming may perhaps be better suited for male contract labourers (harvesting, for example) than for females who would find it difficult to combine this type of work with household work. Hence the 'withdrawal' of women from the labour force (in low participation areas) is partly voluntary due to status reasons and partly involuntary arising from the incompatibility between household work and the changed requirements of labour. While females from affluent families need not work, poor women are forced to work out of necessity. In households that are neither affluent nor poor, voluntary and involuntary withdrawals from the work force are relative and difficult to distinguish because of changes in the households conditions and the labour market situations such as a nature and duration of work, prevailing wage rates and proximity to the work place.

Jayanthi (1995) said employment is an active, multidimensional process which should enable women to realise their full identity and powers in all spheres of life. It would consist of greater access to knowledge and resource, greater autonomy in decision–making, greater ability to plan their lives, have greater control over the circumstances that influences their lives and free them from shackles imposed on them by custom, belief and practice. Generally, development with justice is expected to generate forces that lead to empowerment of various sections of population in a country and to raise their status.

Das et al. (1996) observed that the women, landless and poor, in India do as much as an 80 per cent of the work of rice cultivation. Women have a predominant role in rice production by pulling the seedling in nursery, transplanting, weeding, harvesting and post-harvest activities. Data generated on activity analysis made in a coastal eco-region of Orissa have revealed that involvement of women in rice production vary with production systems. In Green Revolution production systems, women contribute 100 per cent in transporting, 50 per cent in weeding, 62 per cent in transplanting of harvest from field to threshing yard and 75 per cent in cleaning, drying and storage of grain. In contrast, the share load of women varies in small production systems in uprooting of seedling (20%), transplanting (100%), weeding (30%), harvesting (80%), transporting (20%) and drying (20%).

They also noticed that for rice production, involvement of women is by and large negligible in land preparation and application of chemicals (fertilizer, weedicide and pesticide).

Their input in other activities such as uprooting of seedlings, transplanting, weedings, harvesting, threshing and post-harvest operations are dominant. Consequently, development of technology and adoption of the same by farm women should match their activities. Women based activities are labour intensive that has attracted the scientists to develop time efficient implements and machines for reducing the drudgery. Operation of a rice transplanter is a male oriented job, requiring muscle power. Although availability of labour is becoming a problem, use of transplanter, labour saving fast job oriented device, will make many women labourers out of job. The possible solution for such a situation is to develop transplanter that can be operated by women. Manually operated weeders, now available, can be handled by women which will help to reduce drudgery in weeding operation for upland rice.

Kishwar (1996) expressed that various studies have shown that women's work days are ate least twice as long as men's. In rural areas, women combine farm works with house-work. Most women are not even respected for the 15 to 16 hours of daily toil and drudgery in order to keep the family going. They need better nutrition and less drudgery every day of the week not just once in a while.

Parthasarathy (1996) observed that the gender issue has figured prominently in the discussions on employment and wages. It is suggested that modern growth process marginalises female labour and makes them more dependent on male heads. The evidence also shows that income of the women is spent on household and children much more than the income of the males.

Charu Lata. (1997) observed that women spent long hours with much labour in repetitive operations resulting in fatigue and drudgery. Therefore, the life of women is full of drudgery at every stage. According to her, on an average a woman devoted 25-73 man days as against only 11.64 man days devoted by a man in cultivation of one acre of paddy. It is also revealed that educated respondents use to undertake lower drudgery load as they had employed casual of permanent labour for paddy cultivation operations in the area of Haryana, due to which the drudgery undertaken by them reduced considerable. Women besides shouldering almost entire work load by household activities, child rearing and substantial contribution in farming, were found to work in the field for more hours than men folk.

Godara (1997) revealed that women have maximum participation in picking cotton, followed by storing, sowing, plant protection and manuring. While they have no participation in irrigation preparatory tillage and marketing.

Khandekar and Kunru (1997) found that decisions regarding economic activity like cattle, buffalo and goat enterprises were made jointly by a tribal woman and her spouse in Madhya Pradesh. She further discussed decisions, like family nutrition, are taken alone by tribal woman, whereas the outdoor decisions are taken by their husbands alone.

It is imperative that involvement and drudgery is bound to be influenced in either way by the profile of respondents, which might act as facilitator or hindering factor.

Chattopadhyaya (1998) held the view that appropriate technology implies such technology that is suited to the economic and social conditions of practitioners and is in consonance with the level of civilization of the population. One has to seed such technology against waste of resources, destruction of environment and disturbance of the socio-cultural equilibrium. This technology is essential, since traditional ones are not competitive and cannot assure adequate livelihood. A host to activities, can thus, be generated by processing local resources like soil and stones, crops, agricultural wastes, leaves, seeds, barks, fruits, flowers, gums, etc. besides grass herbs and shrubs, mushrooms, etc. The task of livelihood generation, thus, centres on new activities through adoption of appropriate technology, value addition and, hence, viable enterprise generation.

Ethelebert (2000) observed that role of women is gaining importance both from society and government but constitutional and legislative guarantees do not ensure that women will be protected form acts of violence in the family and on the street. Women are the world's caretakers of the home and they play significant role in families and they are the real resource managers.

Sharma and Ogale (2000) noticed that women's active involvement in decision-making is essential for rapid economic development of any country. The success of planned change programmes largely depends on the rational decision-making by women. They were of the opinion that rural women who share abundant responsibilities and perform a wide spectrum of duties in management of households should be given equal power in decision-making process.

Ghosh (2001) observed that even though the adoption of recommended farming technologies gives high production and income to the farmers, yet many of them are reluctant to accept those technologies due to some limitations. These limitations can be broadly classified into (i) technical (ii) economic (iii) socio-psychological and (iv) infrastructural/administrative. Delineation of constraints under each category responsible in adopting the recommended technologies.

According to Executive Summary (2002), tenth five year plan (2002-07), reported that as the ownership of livestock is more evenly distributed with landless labourers and marginal farmers, the progress in animal husbandry sector will result in a more balanced development of the rural economy, particularly in the reduction of poverty ratio. Even many small and medium farmers who derive yearly savings from agriculture are dependent on livestock, especially dairy and poultry for daily subsistence.

Panhwar (2003). In Pakistan, women are not paid for producing crops. They are fed, clothed and provided dowry by father at time of, marriage, ornaments from cradle to gave and not mourned as men are. The men's attitude toward the social set up in the house has changed some what and are a little more considerate but, time may bring about further changes.

CHAPTER 3

Experimental Details

This chapter deals with the research methods and techniques used in the present study. The chapter has been organised in the following sections :-

1. Locale of the study
2. Sampling technique
3. Selection of the variables
4. Operationalization of the variables
5. Data collection
6. Statistical techniques

LOCALE OF THE STUDY

The study was conducted in the two western districts of Uttar Pradesh. This state has been chosen for the study because it is a major state of the country and rural women have a significant role to play in the development of the state as well as the country.

At present Uttar Pradesh state has four economic zones on the basis of cropping pattern, climatic conditions, soil type, etc. the four zones are viz. Western, Central, Eastern and Bundelkhand. The selected two districts fall under Western zone. These districts have been selected purposively since they have higher cropping intensities among all the districts of this zone. The cropping intensity of Rampur district was 102.1 and of Bulandshahr was 100.03 at the time of selection (1996).

SAMPLING TECHNIQUE

For selection of women respondent, a multi-stage sampling procedure has been adopted. According to this procedure, at first stage, 'n' units are selected randomly out of 'N' and then 'm' second stage units are selected out of the first stage selected units in the sample, and so on.

Table 3.1 Selection of households

District	Sampling stage		
	I Block	II Village	III No. of households
Bulandshahr	Sikandarabad	Rithauli	10
		Bainipar	10
		Mandaur	10
		Bhatpura	10
		Khaguabas	10
	Lakhavati	Jamnathere	10
		Akrabad Kuda	10
		Alamgirpur Nainsukh	10
		Jeevat	10
		Mirzapur Agarpur	10
Rampur	Bilaspur	Durzanpur	10
		Parava	10
		Hareya Khurd	10
		Ram Nagaiya	10
		Nagaria Kala	10
	Swar	Prithvi Nagar	10
		Madyan Bhanjan	10
		Milak Kazi	10
		Milak khan	10
		Milak Asad Khan	10

Here for this study, at first stage two blocks from each purposively selected district have been selected and then from each block, five villages have been randomly selected at second stage. At third stage, a list of rural households for reach selected village was prepared. The households then grouped into four categories on the basis of land holding. From each list, 10 households have been selected in proportion to the number of households falling under each category. Thus, in all 200 households have been selected from 20 villages of 4 blocks in two districts.

SELECTION OF THE VARIABLES

The relevant variables for the present study were selected on the basis of extensive review of relevant literature and consultation with experts of the subject.

Table 3.2 Selected variables and their measurements

Variable	Measurement
(A) Independent variables	
1. Socio-personal variables	
(a) Age	Chronological age of the respondents in year.
(b) Caste	SES scale of Trivedi (1963)
(c) Education of respondents	-do-
(d) Social participation	-do-
(e) Family education	SES scale of Trivedi (1963) with necessary modification
(f) Family size	SES scale of Trivedi (1963)
(g) Family type	-do-
(h) House type	SES scale of Trivedi (1963) with necessary modification
(i) Income	Schedule developed for the purpose
(j) Occupation	SES scale of Trivedi (1963)
(k) Land holding	-do-
(l) Martial status of respondent	-do-

(contd.)

Variable	Measurement
2. Economic variables	
(a) Farm powers	Modified SES scale of Trivedi (1963)
(b) Milch animals	Schedule developed for the purpose
(C) Materials possession	Modified SES scale of Trivedi (1963)
(d) Agricultural implements	-do-
(B) Dependent variables	
(a) Knowledge level of women for agricultural, animal husbandry and home technologies	Schedule developed for the purpose
(b) Interest level of women for agricultural, animal husbandry and home technologies	-do-
(c) Adoption level of women for agricultural, animal husbandry and home technologies	-do-
(d) Role of women in agriculture, animal husbandry and household activities	-do-
(e) Decision-making pattern	-do-
(f) Drudgery index	-do-
(g) Efficient agricultural and animal husbandry technologies	-do-
(h) Income generating agricultural and animal husbandry technologies	-do-

OPERATIONALIZATION OF THE VARIABLES

For empirical measurement of the selected variables, the variables are operationalised in the following manner.

(A) Independent variables

(I) Socio-personal variables

(a) Age

The age of the respondent and other members of her family was recorded in years at the time of enquiry. The age of the respondent is further classified and score value was assigned for study purpose as-

	Age	Score
(i)	20-35 years	3
(ii)	36-50 years	2
(iii)	50-65 years	1

The range of age of respondents was between 20 and 65 years.

(b) Caste

Caste was measured by the SES scale of Trivedi (1963) by assigning score:-

Caste	Score
Scheduled caste	1
O.B.C.	2
Upper caste	3

(c) Education of respondents

It is the academic qualifications of the respondents acquired through formal schooling training. The educational level was quantified by giving scores as-

Educational level	Score
Uneducated	0
Up to primary	1
Up to secondary	2
Up to graduate	3

Technical/vocational	4
Above graduate	5

(d) Social participation

It refers to the degree of involvement of respondents in social organisation. It is a voluntary sharing of person to group and group to group relationships, beyond the immediate households. It is quantified on the basis of scoring as-

Participation level	Score
No participation	0
Member of one organization	1
Member of more than one organization	2
Office bearer	3

(e) Family education

It refers to the academic qualifications possessed by the members of the family through formal a schooling and trainings. The years of schooling of different family members were quantified by assigning of scores as per SES scale of Trivedi (1963).

$$\text{Family educational scores} = \frac{\text{Total education score of the family}}{\text{Total number of eligible members of the family}}$$

On the basis of procedure mentioned above, family educational scores were computed and then educational status was determines as –

Status	Percentage of total scores
Low	Up to 33
Medium	34-66
High	67-100

(f) Family-size

It refers to total number of members in the family consisting of husband, wife, children and other dependents. A family consisting of five members and less was considered as small family and a family with more than five members was considered a large family. The scores assigned as per SES scale of Trivedi (1963) were as-

Family size	Score
Up to 5 members	1
More than 5 members	2

(g) Family type

The social group consisting of several related individual families residing in a single large dwelling. Operationally, joint family is applied to those families having at least two married couples, living in common residence and where males are related as father, son or as brothers and earnings from all sources are pooled together and managed by family head. The term nuclear family is applies to those families which consist primarily husband, wife and their children.

The type of family was measured by SES scale of Trivedi (1963) by assigning scores as:-

Family type	Score
Nuclear family	1
Joint family	2

(h) House type

The houses of the respondents were categorised and scores were assigned as :-

Type of house	Score
Katcha	1
Mixed	2
Pucca	3

(i) Income

For the study, income was referred to as the annual monetary income received by the respondent and her family. from all sources. It is measured in terms of rupees.

(j) Occupation

It refers to the main source of livelihood. Occupation was measured by the SES scale of Trivedi (1963) and scores were assigned as-

Occupation	Score
Non-agricultural labourers	0
Caste occupation	1
Farming	2
Business	3
Service	4

(k) Land holding

It refers to the acreage of cultivated land possessed by an individual family. The scores assigned as-

Land holding	Score
No land	0
Up to 1 ha	1
Up to 2 ha	2
Above 2 ha	3

(l) Martial status

The scores were assigned as-

Martial status	Score
Married	2
Widow/Divorcee	1
Unmarried	0

(2) Economic variables

(a) Farm powers

It refers to the actual animal draught power or tractor possessed by the respondent for the use in various farm operations at his/her farm. The scores assigned were as-

Farm power	Score
Up to 2 draught animals	1
Up to 4 draught animals	2
Above 4 draught animals	3
Tractor	6

(b) Milch animals

It refers to total number of milch animals possessed by the family. The scores assigned were as-

Number of milch animals	Score
Up to 2	1
Up to 4	2
Up to 6	3
Above 6	4

(c) Material possession

For this study, it included different types of items. The scores assigned to the following categories:-

(i) Less prestigious items	1
(ii) Medium prestigious items	2
(iii) High Prestigious items	3

According to the above, the scores are as-

Items	Score
Table	1
Chair	1
Sofaset	1
Sewing machine	1
Radio	1
TV	3
Double bed	1

Stove	1
Gas burner	1
Solar cooker	3
Washing machine	3
Cooler	3
Car	3
Motor cycle/scooter	2
Bullock-cart	1
Other items	-

(d) Agricultural implements

The possession of agricultural implements by family was measured in terms of quantity of items. The scores assigned were as-

(i) Up to 4 items	4
(ii) Above 4 items	5
(iii) Tractor driven implements	6

(B) Dependent variables

(C) (a) Knowledge level

Knowledge occurs when an individual is exposed to the innovations existence and gains some understanding of how it function (Rogers, 1962). In the present study, it was operationalised as the totality of understood information possessed by a person. The binary scores assigned to the dichotomized response. The total scores of each respondent was further categorised as-

Knowledge level	Percentage of total score
Poor	Up to 33
Fair	34-66
Good	67-100

(b) Interest level

Interest is the perception of the relationship between two elements of purposeful behaviour, i.e. the present status of a person in some ongoing activity in which he/she is involved and the outcome. The interest is measured on 3- continuum scale as-

Interest level	Scale value
Like	+1
Indifferent	0
Dislike	-1

(c) Adoption

According to Rogers (1962), it is a decision to make full use of an innovation as the best course of action available. It is the mental process through which individual possess from first hearing about innovation to final adoption. Adoption is of two type: (I) behavioural and (ii) cognitive. Behavioural adoption is observed by the number of practices actually put into practice whereas cognitive adoption involves complex decision and changes including obtaining knowledge, critically evaluating practice in terms of individual situation (Ramsey et al., 1959). Here in this study, behavioural adoption has been taken into consideration and adoption index for agricultural technologies was calculated by the following expression:-

$$\text{Adoption index} = \frac{\text{Number of practices ticked}}{\text{Total number of applicable practices}}$$

Adoption level has also been calculated for agricultural technologies as-

Full adoption	–	More than 66 per cent of total number of practices adopted
Partial adoption	–	Less than 66 per cent of total number of practices adopted
No adoption	–	Adoption of no practices

For animal husbandry and home technologies, adoption of practices was assessed by frequency of their use by the respondent. It is measured as-

Frequency of use	Score
Regular	2
Sometimes	1
Never	0

(d) Role of women

Role of women in farm operations, animal husbandry operations and household activities was calculated as-

Dominating role	-	More than 60 per cent of total work performed
Supporting role	-	33 – 65 per cent of total work performed
No role	-	No work is performed

Involvement and time spent by women in farm, animal husbandry and domestic operations have also been assessed.

(e) Decision-making pattern

Decision-making is a mental process, based on conscious reasoning. In this study, it refers to the extent of participation by husband and wife in making decision in all the important matter of home and farm. It is measured by developing schedule for this purpose.

(f) Drudgery index

According to psychologists, physical strains and hardship experienced by human beings is drudgery. In this study, drudgery index was calculated for farm and animal husbandry operations by the use of 'Method of Paired Comparisons: (Edwards, 1969). For preparing drudgery index, a semi-projective type instrument in pictorial form was developed. Only those operations have been selected for calculation of drudgery index which are performed by at least 60 per cent of the total respondents under study. Thus, five farm operations, viz.

weeding, transplanting, harvesting, sowing behind the plough and carrying fodder, feed preparation, milching, fodder chaffing, and preparation of cow dung cakes were selected for drudgery index calculation.

In order to calculate drudgery indices, for each five practices depicted in five pictures, possessing unknown degree of drudgery, were shown in pairs to 30 women respondents. All possible pairs of pictures were made which cam e to be 10 [nc2]. Each pair was then shown to the 30 respondents to make a judgement about the degree of drudgery involved in the operations depicted in the pairs of pictures in comparative terms i.e. high low. For paired comparison, as suggested by Edwards (1969), 'F', 'p' and 'z' matrices were prepared which yielded scores indicating relative degree of drudgery involved in the selected practices.

Thurstone's Law of Comparative Judgement assumes that for a given stimulus I there is associated a most frequently aroused or model discriminal process on a psychological continuum. The mean or medium discriminal process associated with stimulus I is taken as the scale value of the stimulus.

It is assumed that the distribution of discriminal process for two stimuli, I and j, are normal. The difference between two normally distributed variables is also normally distributed as-

$$\sigma_{i-j} = \sqrt{\sigma_i^2 + \sigma_j^2 - 2r_{ij}\sigma_i\sigma_j}$$

The scale separation between two s_i and s_j and the value of normal deviate (Z_{ij}) corresponding to the proportion of comparative judgements (p_{ij}) is as-

$$\bar{S}_i - \bar{S}_j = Z_{ij}\sqrt{\sigma_i^2 + \sigma_j^2 - 2r_{ij}\sigma_i\sigma_j}$$

Or

$$Z_{ij} = \frac{\bar{S}_i - \bar{S}_j}{\sqrt{\sigma_i^2 + \sigma_j^2 - 2r_{ij}\sigma_i\sigma_j}}$$

According to case V model of Law of Comparative Judgement

$$Z_{ij} = \bar{S}_i - \bar{S}_j$$

If the discrepancies between the empirical pij and the theoretical pij values seem unusually large and if the Chi-square test for goodness of fit indicates that the Case V model does not apply, new scale values of stimuli are calculated by using Case III model as

$$\bar{S}_i - \bar{S}_j = Z_{ij} \cdot \sqrt{\sigma_i^2 + \sigma_j^2 - 2r_{ij}\sigma_i\sigma_j}$$

Before applying Case III model, the stimuli were checked for circular triads as-

$$\xi = 1 - \frac{24d}{n^3 - n} \text{ when n is odd}$$

and

$$\xi = 1 - \frac{24d}{n^3 - 4n} \text{ when n is even}$$

In the present study, n = 5 i.e. odd value, so the maximum number of circular triads will be –

$$\frac{n^3 - n}{24} = \frac{(5^3 - 5)}{24} = 5$$

and

$$\xi = 0$$

It shows there is no circular triads.

(g) Efficiency

It refers to the production efficiency of agricultural and animal husbandry technologies. The efficiency score was calculated on 5 continuum scale value as-

Efficiency	Scale value
Least efficient	1
A little efficient	2
Efficient	3
More efficient	4
Most efficient	5

(h) Income generating

It refers to the income generating agricultural and animal husbandry technologies. The score was calculated on 5 continuum scale as-

Income	Scale value
Not increasing	0
Least increasing	1
Less increasing	2
More increasing	3
Most increasing	4

DATA COLLECTION

The data were collected by personally interviewing the selected respondents of both the districts with the help of a structural schedule. The schedule was prepared after consultation and discussion with experts of the field. It consists all the objectives and dimensions of the study. The data collection was accomplished during 1999.

STATISTICAL TECHNIQUES

The following statistical techniques have been applied in the analysis of data:-

Average

It is defined as the sum of the observations divided by its number. If $X_1, X_2, X_3 \ldots X_N$ and N observations then average is as

$$\bar{X} = \frac{\Sigma X}{N}$$

For calculating average score, weighted average formula was used. If n_1 is number of participants and X_i is scale value, then

$$\text{Av. score} = \frac{\Sigma n_i X_i}{\Sigma n_i}$$

Variance

It is defined as the mean of the squares of the deviation taken from arithmetic mean. The expression is as

$$\sigma_2^i = \frac{\Sigma(X - \bar{X})^2}{n - 1}$$

The square root of variance is known as Standard Deviation.

Level of significance

The maximum probability of rejecting the hypothesis when it is true or the maximum probability of Type I error is known as level of significance. The level of significance is denoted by '-' and for moderate precision it is taken as 0.05 and for high precision it is taken a 0.001.

P- value

Another approach for adjudging significance of H_0 is P-value. If P-value is less than or equal to -, the H_0 is rejected, otherwise accept Ho.

$P \leq \alpha$ H_0 rejected

$P \geq \alpha$ H_0 accepted

Coefficient of variability

It is calculated for determining the variation in adoption as:

$$\text{Coefficient of variability} = \frac{\text{highest adoption} - \text{Lowest adoption}}{\text{Highest adoption} + \text{lowest adoption}}$$

Tests of significance

In empirical research, in order to determine the acceptability of hypothesis which is derived form the theories, tests of significance is applied. First a null-hypotheses (H_0), which is usually formulated for the purpose of being rejected, is selected and then suitable statistical test for its testing (H_0) through a set of empirical data would be applied.

Correlation coefficient

Karl Pearson has given a coefficient of correlation for the measurement of linear relationship which exists between two variables. If X and Y are two variables and if E (X,Y) = 0 then correlation coefficient (r) is

$$r = \frac{\text{Cov.}(X, Y,)}{\sqrt{\text{Var.}(X).\ \text{Var.}(Y)}}$$

or

$$= \frac{\Sigma xy}{\sqrt{\Sigma x^2 \cdot \Sigma y^2}}$$

where,

$$\Sigma xy = \left[\Sigma XY - \frac{\Sigma X \Sigma Y}{n}\right]$$

$$\Sigma x^2 = \left[\Sigma X^2 - \frac{(\Sigma X)^2}{n}\right]$$

$$\Sigma y^2 = \left[\Sigma Y^2 - \frac{(\Sigma Y)^2}{n}\right]$$

and n = Sample size

Here, one variable is dependent on other. For testing the significance of correlation coefficient (r). T test is applied. Degree of lack of relationship or coefficient of alienation is measures as-

$$K = \sqrt{1 - r^2}$$

Rank correlation coefficient

When numbers or other symbols are used simply to classify an object or characteristic, non-parametric measures of correlation are used which male no assumption about the shape of the population from which the scores have been drawn. Spearman's rank correlation (rs) is a measure of association which requires that both the variables be measured in at least on ordinal scale so that the object or characteristic understudy may be ranked in two ordinal series. The formula for measurement of association is-

$$r_s = \frac{6\Sigma d_i^2}{(n^3 - n)}$$

Where d is deviation between two variables and n is sample size.

t-test

This test is applied when the sample size is small. When samples are small and independent and their population variances are homogeneous. Fisher's t-test is applied.

(I) When $n_1 \neq n_2$

The formula for t-test is

$$t = \frac{|\bar{x}_1 - \bar{x}_2|}{\sqrt{S^2[1/n_1 + 1/n_2]}}$$

Where,

$$S^2 = \text{Pooled variance} = \frac{(n_1 1)S_1^2 + (n_2 1)S_2^2}{n_1 + n_2 - 2}$$

$$= \frac{\Sigma x_1^2 + \Sigma x_2^2}{n_1 + n_2 - 2}$$

$$\Sigma x_1^2 = \Sigma x_1^2 - (\Sigma X_1)^2 / n_1$$

$$\Sigma x_2^2 = \Sigma x_2^2 - (\Sigma X_2)^2 / n_2$$

If t cal. t tab, at α level of significance with $(n_1 + n_2 - 2)$ d.f., H_0 is rejected.

(2) When $n_1 = n_2 = n$, the formula will become

$$t = \frac{|\bar{x}_1 - \bar{x}_2|}{\sqrt{S^2[1/n + 1/n]}} = \frac{|\bar{x}_1 - \bar{x}_2|}{\sqrt{S^2[2/n]}}$$

If t-cal. > t-tab, at α level of significance with 2(n - 1) d.f., H_0 is rejected.

(3) For testing significance of correlation coefficient; t-test is applied in the following manner.

$$t = \frac{(r - 0)\sqrt{n-2}}{\sqrt{1 - r^2}}$$

If t-cal. t-tab, at ... level of significance with (n-2) d.f., the null hypothesis that p = 0 will be rejected.

Z-test

(1) For proportions

When there are two population of individuals (or objects) having the same proportion, P of possessing a particular character, it is to test whether the proportions in the samples are significantly different form each other or not.

Let $p_1 = x_1/n_1$ and $p_2 = x_2/n_2$ are the two proportions of individuals possessing the dame attribute in the samples of sizes n_1 and n_2, respectively. Assuming that populations are normal and samples are drawn independently and at random, the test used is as-

$$Z = \frac{|p_1 - p_2|}{\sqrt{P_0 Q_0 [1/n_1 + 1/n_2]}}$$

If Z cal. ≥ Z tab. at α level of significance, the H_0 ($P = P_0$) is rejected. It means there is significant difference between the two proportions in the samples. In other words, their populations are having the sample proportion (P_0).

(2) For homogeneity of correlations

For testing the null hypothesis ($P_1 = P_2$), Fisher's Z-transformation is applied in the following manner.

$$Z_1 = \frac{1}{2} \log_e \frac{1 + r_1}{1 - r_1}$$

and

$$Z_2 = \frac{1}{2} \log_e \frac{1 + r_2}{1 - r_2}$$

Here r_1 and r_2 are the sample correlation coefficients for the Ist and 2nd samples. Z-test for testing difference between Z_1 and Z_2 is applied as-

$$Z = \frac{|Z_1 - Z_2|}{\sqrt{(1/n_1 - 3) + (1/n_2 - 3)}}$$

Where, n1 and n2 are sample sizes of two populations.

If Z-cal. > Z-tab. At ... level of significance, the H0 is rejected.

Chi-square test

This test is applied for testing the agreement between observed and expected frequencies when frequencies fall in different classes. This test is applied for enumeration of data which generally relate to discrete variable. The formula for Chi-square test is as-

$$\chi^2 = \Sigma\left[\frac{(O - E)^2}{E}\right]$$

Where O = Observed frequency

E = Expected frequency

If χ^2 cal. > χ^2 tab at α level of significance with (r – 1) (c – 1) d.f., the H0 that two attributes are independent is accepted.

For testing significance for the Case V model of paired comparison method, the test is applied as–

$$\chi^2 = \left[\frac{\Sigma(\theta - \theta')^2}{821/N}\right]$$

Where, $\theta = \text{arc Sin}\sqrt{p}$

N = Number of judgements upon which p is based

If χ^2 cal. < χ^2 tab at α level of significance with (n – 1) (n – 2)/2 d.f., the H_0 is accepted that statements are tenable.

Analysis of variance

This technique is useful in testing the differences between two or more means. In this technique, total variation in a variable can be reduced into different component associated with possible sources of variability whose relative importance we wish to assess.

When we consider two factors or variables simultaneously for study, the two way analysis of variance is used. In case of one observation per cell, the analysis of variance is as given below;

Sources of variance	d.f.	S.S.	M.S.	F
Between A levels	(n-1)	SSA	SSA/(n-1)	SSA(m-1)/SS1
Between B levels	(m-1)	SSB	SSB/(m-1)	SSB(n-1)/SS1
Interaction (AXB)	(n-1)(m-1)	SS1	SS1/(n-1)(m-1)	
Total	(nm-1)	T.S.S.		

If F cal. > F tab. At ...level of significance, the H0 is rejected, there is no difference between two variances.

Diversity Index

For nominal scale data, there is no mean or median to serve as a reference for discussion of dispersion. Instead wee can invoke the concept of diversity. The quantitative expression appropriate as a measure of diversity for nominal data is-

$$H = \frac{n \log n - \Sigma fi \log fi}{n}$$

Where,

Fi = frequency of the category

N = sample size

K = number of categories

It is known as Shannon's Index of diversity. The maximum possible diversity for a set of data consisting K categories is (H max – log K) and relative diversity is

$$J = \frac{H}{H\,max} = \frac{n \log n - \Sigma fi \log fi}{n - \log k}$$

J may be termed as homogeneous or evenness. The test for difference between two diversity indices is-

$$T = \frac{H_1 - H_2}{SE_{(H_1 - H_2)}}$$

Where $SE_{(H_1-H_2)} = \sqrt{S_{H_1}{}^2 + S_{H_2}{}^2}.$

The d.f. associated with t-test is

$$\nu = \frac{(S_{H_1}{}^2 + S_{H_2}{}^2)}{\left[\frac{S_{H_1}{}^2}{n_1} + \frac{S_{H_2}{}^2}{n2}\right]}$$

Here,

$$S^2_{H_i} = \frac{1}{N^2}\left[\Sigma fi^2 \log fi^2 - \frac{(\Sigma fi \log fi^2)}{n}\right]$$

CHAPTER 4

Profile of the Study Area

Prior to discuss the findings of the study on role and status of rural women, it is essential to sketch briefly the salient features of the study area. The following is the brief features of the districts Bulandshahr and Rampur.

DISTRICT BULANDSHAHR

The district had received its name form the *Banchhati* (land recovered from forests), Naranavata, Baran and Unchangar as being situated on the high edge of the valley of Kali Nadi well above the level of the surrounding country. The present name was Persianised in mediaeval times.

Location

The district occupies the southern most part of the Merrut division and lies between latitude 28°4'N and 28°40'N and longitude 77°18'E and longitude 78°28'E. It is, bounded on the north by district Ghaziabad on the east Jyotiba Phule Nagar and Bandaun, on the south district Aligarh and on the west district Gautam Budh Nagar.

Geographical area

According to Central Statistical Organisation, the geographical area of the district was 4895 sq. km during 1971 but it has reduced to 3458 sq. km during 1991 when some districts of the Uttar Pradesh have been reorganised.

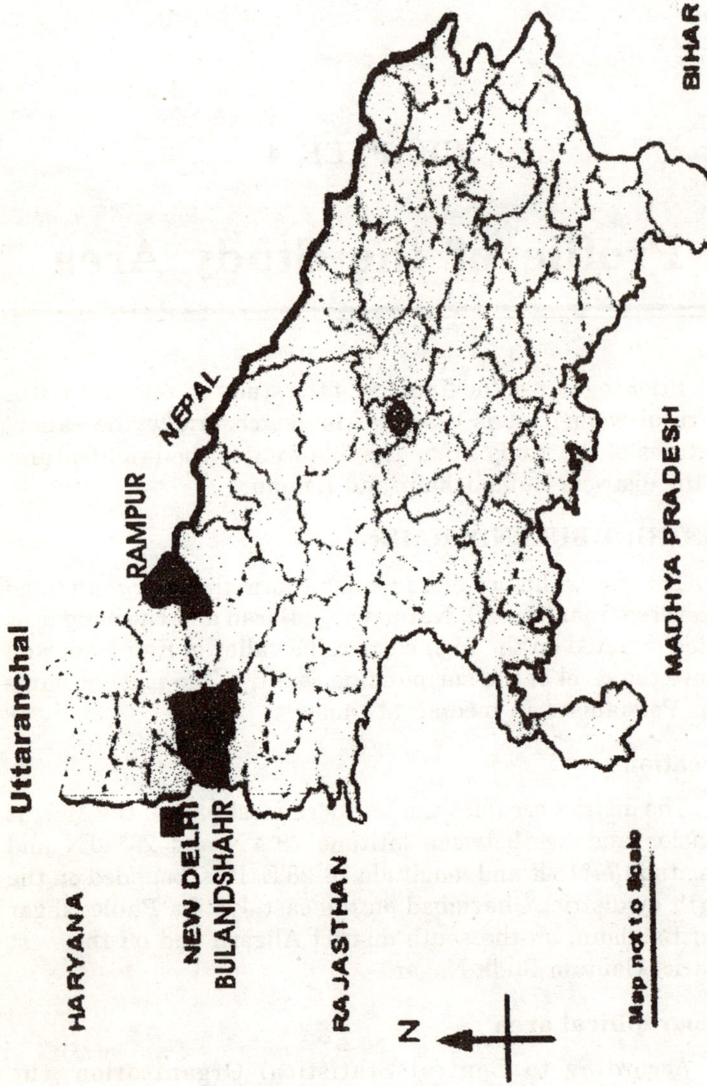

Uttar Pradesh

LAKHAWATI BLOCK

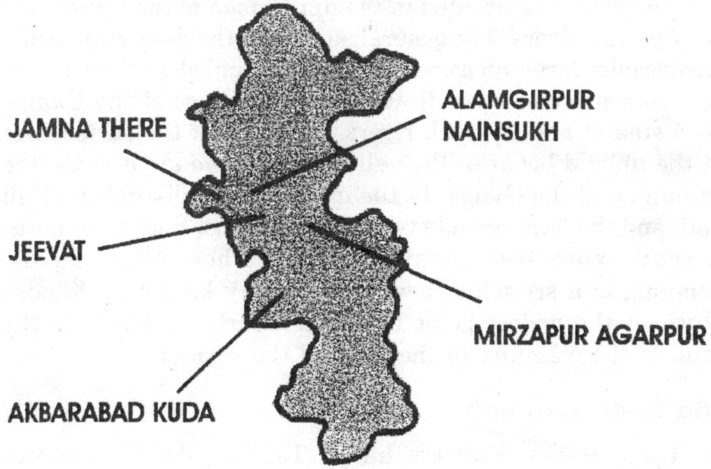

SIKANDARABAD BLOCK

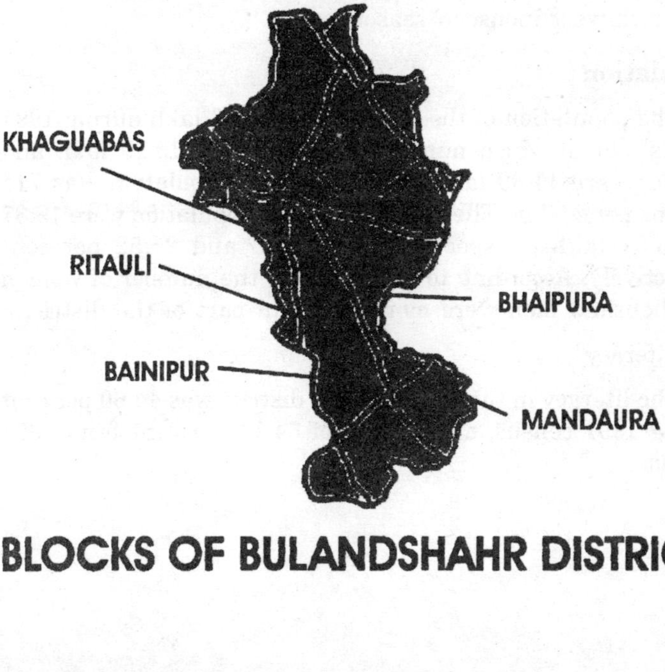

BLOCKS OF BULANDSHAHR DISTRICT

Topography

The district is situated in the upper *doab* of the Ganga and the Yamuna rivers. The general surface of the district presents a uniformity level appearance with a gradual slope from north-west to south-east as indicated by the courses of the Ganga, the Yamuna and the Kali rivers. The bulk of the surface lies on the upland between the valleys of the two great rives, the Yamuna and the Ganga. In the middle of the district the Kali Nadi and the Nim provide two main drainage lines from north to south which run parallel to each other. Adjoining the Yamuna, is a stretch of low lying country known as Khadar which at the widest point measures nearly 16 km from the bank of the Yamuna to the crest of the upland.

Administrative units

The present districts has 7 Tahsils, 15 Community Development Blocks and 1195 villages out of which 1122 villages were populated during 1999.

Climate

The climate of the district is characterised by a cold weather, a hot summer and general dryness, except during the south-west monsoon season.

Population

The population of the district was 24.68 lakh during 1991 census, out of which number of males were 13.29 lakh and females were 11.39 lakh. The density of population was 714 persons per sq. km. The rural and urban population were 19.37 and 5.31 lakhs, respectively i.e. 78.48 and 21.52 per cent respectively. According to 1991 census, the number of women per thousand men were more in urban part of the district.

Literacy

The literacy in the Bulandshahr district was 44.60 per cent during 1991 census, an increase of 54.11 per cent from 1981 census.

Table 4.1 Population of Bulandshahr district according to 1991 census

Year/Block/Village	Population (lakh)			Percentage		Women over men
	Male	Female	Total	Male	Female	
1971	10.21	8.70	18.91	53.99	46.01	852
1981	12.57	10.96	23.53	53.42	46.58	872
1991	13.29	11.39	24.68	53.85	46.15	857
Rural	10.47	8.90	19.37	54.05	45.95	850
Urban	2.82	2.49	5.31	53.11	46.90	883
Sikandarabad	0.82	0.69	1.51	54.30	45.69	841
Ritauli	-	-	0.012			
Benipur	-	-	0.018			
Mandawarali	-		-	0.024		
Bhatpura	-	-	0.012			
Khaguwas	-	-	0.011			
Lakhawti	0.61	0.53	1.14	53.51	46.49	869
Jamanathour	-	-	0.006			
Akbarabad Kuda	-	-	0.0105			
Alamgirpur nainsukh	-	-	0.008			
Jeevat	-	-	0.018			
Mirzapur Agarpur	-	-	0.006			

Table 4.2 Literacy in Bulandshahr district according to 1991 census

Year/Block	Number of literates			Percentage		
	Male	Female	Total	Male	Female	Total
1971	330532	80883	411415	32.6	9.3	21.84
1981	537376	145811	683187	42.5	13.3	28.94
1991	653959	220963	874922	61.5	24.6	44.60
Urban	146938	81194	228132	64.8	40.9	53.65
Rural	507021	139769	646790	60.6	19.9	42.10
Sikandarabad	43384	12355	55739	66.6	22.7	46.60
Lakhawati	31516	8328	39844	64.1	20.3	44.18

The percentage of male and female literacy were 61.5 and 24.6, respectively. This indicates that in the district males have preponderance over females in literacy. Regarding Sikandarabad and Lakhawati blocks too literacy were between 44 and 46 per cent.

Industry

The old industries of the district were the cotton prints of Jahangirabad, Muslims of Sikandarabad, pottery of Khurja, rugs and carpets of Jewar and wood carving of Bulandshahr and Shikarpur. The goods produced by these industries were of superior quality and had obtained a wide reputation. At present, the district had produced through its 169 working factories a total production of Rs. 911 crores value during 1992-93. There were 13619 villages and small scale industrial units in the district during 1999-2000. Out of this, 1024 units were working in engineering sector, 227 units in chemical sector and 8342 units in handicraft sector.

Land utilization and reclamation

The net sown area during 1998-99 was 281725 hectares which is 77.88 per cent of total projected area. It was noticed that the net sown area in the district has shown a declining trend of 0.55 per cent since 1996-97.

There is a large area in the district which is affected by *reh* and has turned *usar* (barren) where no vegetation thrives nor they are culturable by ordinary methods. The user and wastelands are about 2.53 per cent of the total projected area of the district. Soil erosion is great problem and almost all the Tehsils are affected by it. Nearly one fifth of the total cultivated area of the district is suffering with the problem.

Irrigation

Net irrigated area in the district during 1998-99 was 246287 hectares, less than 12.58 per cent of the net area sown. The irrigated area had varied year to year as it is significantly affected by the adequacy and timeliness of rainfall. The methods of irrigation in the district are canals, tubewells, wells, tanks and other sources. Of the net irrigated area 246287 hectares

202131 hectares area is irrigated by tubewells, 36515 hectares area by canals and 3564 hectares area by wells. There are 476 public tubewells, which irrigates 5.69 per cent area of net irrigated area and 36465 private tubewells.

Table 4.3 Land utilization in Bulandshahr district during 1998-99 (ha)

Land utilization	Blocks		District
	Sikandarabad	Lakhawati	
Projected area	30012	20652	361748
Forest	614	748	16557
Barren land	530	450	6046
Current fallow	857	217	5516
Fallow land	545	674	6764
Usar and Wasteland	1385	516	9136
Land in the use other Than farming	2777	1287	33599
Pastures	341	37	687
Horticulture	93	191	1718
Net sown area	22870	16532	281725
Area sown more than Once	17998	13181	204960
Total cultivated area	40868	29713	486685
Net irrigated area	20364	43423	246287
Total irrigated area	14305	29759	484663

Soil

The chief soil of the district is a rich loam, *seota*. A distinctive feature of this soil is that it dries white or to a very light gray and becomes of dark colour when manured and moistened. It varies in quality, being richer where it is least mixed with sand, and it firm, forming into hard clods.

Harvests

The mode of cultivation in the district is similar to that which prevails throughout in the doab. Harvests are known by the usual names *kharif*, *rabi* and *zaid*. The areas under *kharif* and *Rabi* crops during 1998-99 were 240356 and 222704 hectares, respectively.

Principal crops

In the *kharif* season, maize is among the most important crops, next come jowar and *bajra*. In the *Rabi* season, the most important crop is wheat which forms the main agricultural staple and is also the chief source of prosperity of the peasantry of the district. It is sown alone in poorer lands and it is frequently mixed with gram and barley. Of the total cultivated area (240356 hectares) during *kharif* 1998-99 season, paddy had covered 9.13 per cent maize covered 39.52 per cent and bajra covered 4.02 per cent area. Though maize covered more area than paddy, but the productivity of maize crop (12.53 q/ha) is 79.25 per cent less than that of paddy (22.46 q/ha). During *Rabi* season of 1998-99, the productivity of wheat was 36.37 q/ha, and of barley was 33.82 q/ha. This indicates that barley is the second most important crop of *Rabi* in the district.

Table 4.4 Area, production and productivity of principal crops in Bulandshahr district during 1998-99

Season/crops	Area (ha)		Production (tonnes)	Productivity (q/ha)
	Irrigated	Total		
Kharif				
Paddy	21483	21946	49298.00	22.46
Maize	94467	95218	119256.00	12.52
Jowar	542	543	320.00	5.90
Bajra	9514	9675	11994.00	12.40
Rabi				
Wheat	171976	171976	625440.00	36.37
Barley	15107	15107	51090.00	33.82
Total pulses	19233	19262	10211.00	5.30
Total oilseeds	9113	9113	7359.00	8.08
Total cereals	313089	314465	857398.00	27.26
Total food grains	332322	333727	867609.00	26.00
Sugarcane	42493	42493	2629807.00	618.88

Financial institutions

During 1999-2000, there were 130 branches of nationalised banks, 10 branches of rural banks and only two branches of non-nationalized banks. The Sikandarabad and Lakhawati blocks were having three and five branches of nationlised banks, respectively. Six branches of rural banks were situated in the rural areas and of this one each at Sikandarabad and Lakhawati was situated. The total money deposited during 1999-2000 was Rs. 38.34 lakh i.e. 32 per cent of the total deposit. About 61.98 per cent of total loan distributed during 1999-2000 was distributed to agriculture and its allies.

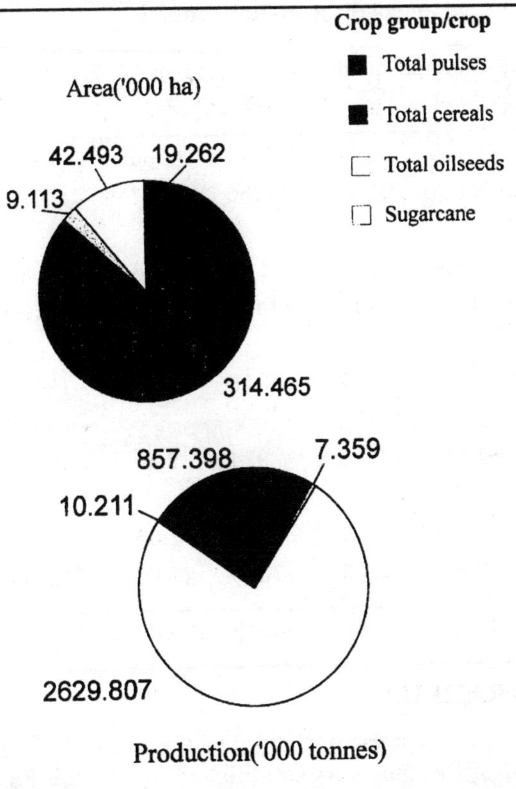

Fig.4.1: Area and production of principal crops in Bulandshahr district during 1998-99

There were 145 agricultural loan cooperative societies which have 233674 members and working capital Rs. 2714.51 lakh during 1999-2000. Of 145 cooperative societies, Sikandarabad and Lakhawati blocks were having 5 and 13 societies, respectively.

Occupational structure

The occupation-wise distribution of the population of Bulandshahr shows that there were 41.46 per cent farmers and 20.18 per cent agricultural labourers, according to 1991 census. It was 17.9 per cent of total population in the district.

Table 4.5 Occupational structure in Bulandshahr district according to 1991 census

Occupation	Sikandarabad		Lakhawati		District	
	No.	%	No.	%	No.	%
Farmers	19418	43.47	18674	53.60	296724	41.46
Agricultural Labourers	9119	20.41	5356	15.37	144391	20.18
Family labour	504	1.13	340	0.98	11980	1.67
Non-family Labour	3652	8.17	1476	4.24	45190	6.31
Construction Work	745	1.67	315	0.90	11004	1.54
Trade and Commerce	1208	2.71	974	2.80	50329	7.04
Transport	934	2.09	368	1.05	14775	2.06
Others	9092	20.35	7340	21.06	141235	19.74
Total	44672	100.00	34843	100.00	715628	100.00

DISTRICT RAMPUR

Rampur is an historical district of Uttar Pradesh. During 1774, *riyasat* of Rampur was established by Nawab Faizullah Khan. This *riyasat* had seen several turmoils and at last on 1st July, 1949, *riyasat* was absorbed into Indian Union.

Location

The district lies between 78°54' and 69°28' east longitude and 28°25' and 29°18' north latitude. The district is surrounded on north by Nainital, on east by Bareilly, on south by Budayun and on west by Moradabad.

Geographical area

According to Central Statistical Organisation, the geographical area of the district is 2367 sq. km which is only 8.8 per cent of total geographical area of Uttar Pradesh state.

Topography

The district is situated in the *tarai* of Himalyayn. The whole area of the district is surrounded by Ramganga river and minor river like Kosi, Gangan, Sejani and Peelakhar. The soil of the district is fertile and suitable for agriculture. The land inclination is from north to south direction.

Administrative units

The district has 5 Tehsils viz. Bilaspur, Milak, Shahabad, Swar and Rampur and 6 Community Development Blocks viz., Swar, Bilaspur, Saidnagar, Chamaraoa, Sahabad and Milak. There are 1153 villages out of which 1097 are populated villages, 55 are non populated villages and one village is forest village.

Panchayat System

The district has 75 Nayaya Panchayats and 568 Gram Sabha. The total income from Panchayats is Rs. 67308.00 during 1999.

Climate

The climate of the district is characterised by a cold weather, a hot summer and dryness, except during the south-west monsoon season. The average rainfall in the district is approximately 1578 mm.

Population

The population of the district during 1991 census was 15.01 lakh, out of which 8.08 lakh were males and 6.93 lakh were

Swar Block

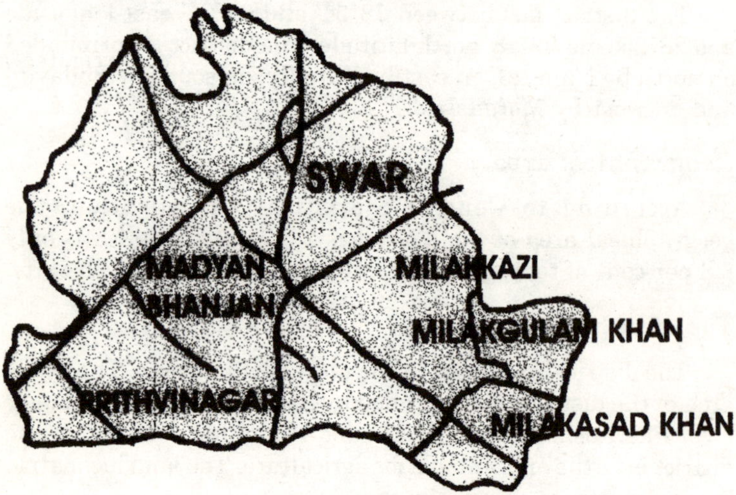

Bilaspur Block

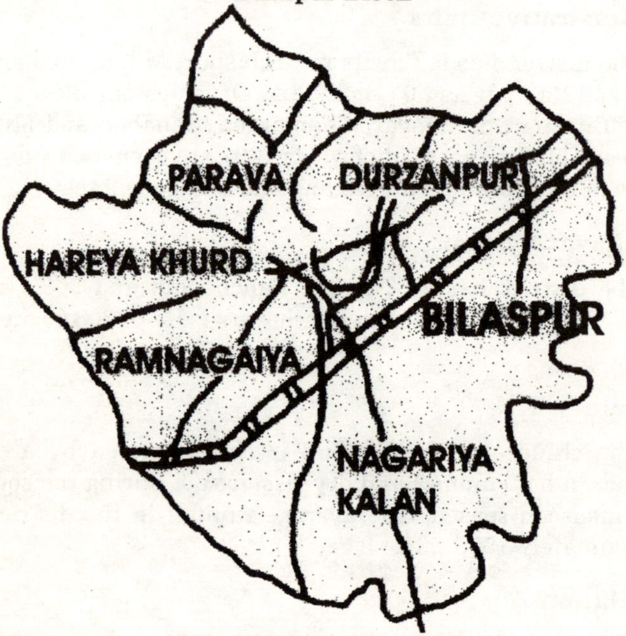

Blocks of Rampur District

females. Population growth during eighties was 27.42 per cent whereas it was 30.78 per cent during seventies. This indicates that population growth in the district is decreasing. The population density during 1981 was 498 persons sq. km. which increased to 635 persons per sq. km. The women per thousand men was 858 and this has increased to 930 during 2001, according to UNDP report.

Table 4.6 Population of Rampur district according to 1991 census

Year/Block/ Village	Population (lakh)			Percentage		Women over men
	M	F	Total	M	F	
1971	4.91	4.10	9.01	54.49	45.51	836
1981	6.39	5.39	11.78	54.29	45.76	843
1991	8.08	6.93	15.01	54.83	46.17	858
Rural	6.01	5.08	11.09	54.19	45.81	846
Urban	2.07	1.85	3.92	52.81	47.19	893
Block Swar	1.45	1.25	2.70	53.70	46.30	862
Prithvi Nagar	-	-	0.017			
Madayan Bhajan	-	-	0.009			
Mikak Kaji	-	-	0.015			
Milak Gulam Khan	-	-	0.012			
Milak Asad Khan	-	-	0.019			
Block Bilaspur	0.79	0.68	1.47	53.74	46.26	860
Durzanpur	-	-	0.006			
Parava	-	-	0.002			
Hareya Khurd	-	-	0.0006			
Ram Nagaiya	-	-	0.001			
Nagaria Kala	-	-	0.011			

Literacy

According to 1991 census, the literacy percentage of the district was 25.4 out of which 33.8 per cent were women and

15.3 per cent were men. This shows that in the district, literacy has increased from 14.3 per cent (1981 census) to 25.4 per cent, yet it is still very low. However, males have preponderance over females in case of literacy, as data indicate. Regarding literacy in the Bilaspur and Swar areas, it has been noted that Bilaspur has 26.7 per cent literate persons while Swar has 18.8 per cent literates.

Table 4.7 Literacy in Rampur district according to 1991 census

Year/Block	Number of literates			Percentage		
	Male	Female	Total	Male	Female	Total
1971	86867	29409	116276	17.7	7.2	12.9
1981	144669	47891	192560	22.7	8.9	16.3
1991	215680	81908	297588	33.8	15.3	25.4
Urban	82970	50843	133813	49.0	34.0	42.0
Rural	132082	30763	162845	28.2	8.0	19.1
Swar	30466	8544	39010	27.1	9.0	18.8
Bilaspur	22364	8377	30741	35.7	16.0	26.7

Industry

Prior to absorption into the state, the place of Rampur was second to Kanpur in case of industrialisation because the riyasat was giving financial assistance to capitalists for establishment of industries in the riyasat. After absorption, on account of some unknown reasons, most of the industries shifted to other parts of state and during 1992-93 there were only 119 working factories with 10424 workers. During 1999-2000 there were 11710 rural and small scale industries in which 41977 workers were working. *Jardozi* work, knife and *Biri* making are main small scale industries of the district.

Land utilization and reclamation

The total projected area of the district during 1998-99 was 235722 hectares out of which net sown area was 193249 hectares (81.98 per cent). The net sown area in the district has decreased from 193783 hectares (1996-97) to 193249 hectares (1998-99), i.e. a decrease of 0.27 per cent was noticed during two years. In spite of decrease in usar land from 370 hectares to 197 hectares, current fallow from 1273 hectares to 707 hectares and other fallow lands from 721 hectares to 301 hectares, the net sown area in the district has witnessed a decrease during 1996-98.

Table 4.8 Land utilization in Rampur district during 1998-99 (ha)

Land utilization	Block		District
	Swar	Bilaspur	
Projected area	52849	51378	235722
Forest	4189	1876	6611
Barren land	42	31	197
Current fallow	-	411	707
Fallow land	-	54	301
Usar and Wasteland	1369	1039	7652
Land in use other than farming	6553	52343	26221
Pastures	2	-	4
Horticulture	66	320	780
Net sown area	42414	40637	193249
Area sown more than Once	38509	37533	160212
Total cultivated area	83065	76655	353461
Net irrigated area	39527	42631	184849
Total irrigated area	76289	75079	330175

Irrigation

The net irrigated area during 1998-99 was 184849 hectares out of which 39527 hectares land was irrigated in Swar block and 42631 hectares land irrigated in Bilaspur block. This shows that 95.65 per cent of net sown area in the district was irrigated during 1998-99. About 75 per cent of total irrigated area was irrigated by private resources. During *Rabi* and Kharif 1998-99, the total cultivated areas were 146871 and 174028 hectares, respectively.

The irrigation resources in the district are canals, tubewells, wells, tanks and other sources. Of the net irrigated area 184849 hectares, 3.34 per cent was irrigated by canals, 0.91 per cent by 327 public tubewells, 94.47 per cent by 52051 private tubewells, 0.49 per cent by wells, 0.42 per cent by tanks and the rest by other sources.

Soil

In most part of the district, loam soil is found which is very fertile and suitable for agriculture. In some part, sandy loam soil is also found.

Principal crops

In *kharif* season, paddy, maize, jowar and bajra are the main crops and in *Rabi* season wheat and barley are the main crops. In cash crops, sugarcane is the main crop of the district. Of the total cropped area (307690 hectares) paddy covers 43.4 per cent, maize covers 0.14 per cent, wheat covers 40.13 per cent and sugarcane covers 8.02 per cent area. Thus, paddy and wheat are main crops of this district.

The productivity of wheat 32.38 quintal/ha and of paddy 18.43 quintal/ha. The productivity of sugarcane was 617.56 quintals/ha and the production during 1998-99 was 15.24 lakh tonnes.

Financial institutions

During 1998-99, there were 60 branches of nationalised banks and 37 branches of rural banks. There was only one branch of non nationalised bank. In Swar block, there were 4 branches of nationalised banks and 9 branches of rural bank whereas in Bilaspur block, there were 7 branches of nationalised banks and 4 branches of rural bank. Total money deposited in the banks were Rs. 43.74 lakh and loan distributed was Rs. 33.31 lakh, out of which Rs. 15.62.lakh was distributed for agricultural and its allied works. For small scale industries, Rs. 3.81 lakh have been distributed as loan among entrepreneurs.

Table 4.9 Area, production and productivity of principal crops in Rampur district during 1998-99

Season/crops	Area (ha)		Production (tonnes)	Productivity (q/ha)
	Irrigated	Total		
Kharif				
Paddy	133439	133561	246172.00	18.43
Maize	56	422	387.00	11.03
Jowar	2	2524	2008.00	7.96
Bajra	2	3641	2541.00	6.98
Rabi				
Wheat	123479	123479	399829.00	32.38
Barley	11	35	83.00	23.82
Total pulses	1377	7069	5416.00	7.66
Total oilseeds	7757	8754	8332.00	9.52
Total cereals	256969	263591	651020.00	24.70
Total food grains	258346	270660	656436.00	24.25
Sugarcane	24583	24675	1523829.00	617.56
Potato	3595	3595	67597.00	188.03

In the district, there were 64 primary agricultural cooperative societies during 1998-99, in which 165039 were members. Total working capital was Rs. 354136 and deposited money was Rs. 34406. Out of 64 agricultural cooperative societies, 8 were in Bilaspur and 17 were in Swar blocks with working capital Rs. 53739 and Rs. 68767, respectively.

Occupational structure

According to 1991 census, total main workers in the population of Rampur district were 29.3 per cent. Of this, 27.9 per cent were from urban and 29.8 per cent from rural areas. In Swar and Bilaspur blocks, 64.07 and 61.14 per cent were farmers, respectively (Table 4.10).

Table 4.10 Occupational structure in Rampur district according to 1991 census

Occupation	Swar		Bilaspur		District	
	No.	%	No.	%	No.	%
Farmers	54913	64.07	28247	61.14	251337	53.98
Agricultural Labourers	17611	20.55	12270	26.56	68158	14.64
Family labour	652	0.76	180	0.39	7487	1.61
Non-family Labour	1743	2.03	1431	3.10	32796	7.04
Construction Work	349	0.41	185	0.40	5480	1.17
Trade and Commerce	1379	1.61	650	1.41	26869	5.77
Transport	380	0.44	502	1.09	11699	2.52
Others	8679	10.13	2732	5.91	61772	13.27
Total	85706	100.00	46197	100.00	465578	100.00

CHAPTER 5

Findings and Discussion

The empirical results and its discussion have been presented in this chapter. For the purpose of convenience, the presentation has been sub-divided under the following heads :-

I. Socio-economic profile.

II. Knowledge and adoption of technologies.

III. Role of women in farm and household activities.

IV. Decision-making pattern in the family.

V. Involvement of women in different socio-economic groups in farm and household activities.

VI. Employment of women in agriculture and non-agriculture sectors.

VII. Identification of appropriate farm technologies.

SOCIO-ECONOMIC PROFILE

Respondent's profile

Age

Age-wise distribution of respondents shows that 18 per cent women of Rampur district were of age-group 20-35 years, 69 per cent women between age-group 36-50 years and 13 per cent women between 50-65 years (Table 5.1). The average age of women of Rampur district was 37 years. Similarly, for Bulandshahr district, the average age of women respondents was 41 years. It means that women when become middle-aged, they, generally, get involved in work be it of household or of outside. Women of this group effectively engaged themselves in income generating work so that they can supplement family income. Kunwar (1993) has also observed that majority of working women were of adult age group.

Table 5.1 Age-wise distribution of respondents

Age-group (years)	Rampur		Bulandshahr		Pooled	
	Frequency	Range	Frequency	Range	Frequency	Range
20-35	18	24.50±3.02	12	28.50±3.17	30	26.10±3.60
36-50	69	38.30±1.61	62	38.76±1.56	131	38.52±1.31
51-65	13	51.00±0.16	26	52.50±1.02	39	52.00±0.78
Total	100	37.46±4.53	100	41.10±4.60	200	39.29±7.61

Education

It is one of the important factors, which accelerates the knowledge of the respondents which in turn accelerates growth and development in farming. It was observed in this study that 46 per cent of total women respondents were having education up to primary level and 18 per cent women up to secondary level (Table 5.2). This indicates that the women respondents were not having that educational standard which is required at present time. In Rampur district, 38 per cent women were uneducated and 37 per cent women were having education up to primary level whereas in Bulandshahr district, it were respectively 26.00 and 55.00 per cent.

Table 5.2 Education-wise distribution of respondents

Educational level	Rampur		Bulandshahr		Pooled	
	Frequency	%	Frequency	%	Frequency	%
Uneducated	38	38.00	26	26.00	64	32.00
Up to Primary	37	37.00	55	55.00	92	46.00
Up top Secondary	19	19.00	17	17.00	36	18.00
Above Secondary	6	6.00	2	2.00	8	4.00
Total	100	100.00	100	100.00	200	100.00

Caste

In rural areas, caste is an important social institution. In order to find out caste composition of women respondents, the caste hierarchy of the study area was analysed. The results show that 41.50 per cent of the total women respondents were of OBC and 35.0 per cent were of Upper castes. Only 23.50 per cent women belonged to SC households (Table 5.3).

Table 5.3 Caste-wise distribution of respondents

Caste group	Rampur		Bulandshahr		Pooled	
	F	%	F	%	F	%
S.C.	28	28.00	19	19.00	47	23.50
O.B.C.	39	39.00	44	44.00	83	41.50
Upper caste	33	33.00	37	37.00	70	35.00
J-value	0.992		0.951			
t-value	0.0016					
P-value	>0.05					

Note: F = Frequency.

The relative diversity (J) shows that there was high caste diversity among the women respondents of both the districts. No significant difference was observed between the diversity indices, it means that distribution of respondents in both the districts was almost of similar pattern.

Income of the respondents

It was observed that 34.00 per cent women respondents were earning annually up to Rs. 1000 and 61.50 per cent women between Rs. 1000-1500 (Table 5.4). The averages of annual income of women respondents of Rampur and Bulandshahr districts were Rs. 705.50 and Rs. 1103.40, respectively. It indicates that a large proportion of respondents was not earning sufficient income to eke out their livelihood and support their family.

Table 5.4 Income-wise distribution of respondents

Income group (Rs.)	Rampur		Bulandshahr		Pooled	
	F	%	F	%	F	%
below 1000	30	30.00	38	38.00	68	34.00
1000-1500	64	64.00	59	59.00	123	61.50
1500 & above	6	6.00	3	3.00	9	4.50
Total	100	100.00	100	100.00	200	100.00

Inter-relationship among age, caste and education variables

The inter-relations among age, caste and education reveal that respondents belonging to OBC households of both the districts were mostly educated. About 40.91 respondents of OBC and 36.84 per cent respondents of S.C. in Bulandshahr district were having education up to primary level whereas 81.08 per cent respondents of Upper castes were having primary level education. The picture in Rampur district is not different from Bulandshahr district (Tables 5.5 and 5.6).

Table 5.5 Inter-relationship among age, caste and education of respondents of Rampur district

Educational level	Age-group (years) 20-35			36-50			51-65			Total
	SC	OBC	UC	SC	OBC	UC	SC	OBC	UC	
Uneducated	3	5	-	11	10	3	2	1	3	38
Up to Primary	2	4	2	9	10	4	-	1	5	37
Up to Secondary	-	2	-	1	4	11	-	-	1	19
Above Secondary	-	-	-	-	2	4	-	-	-	6
Total	5	11	2	21	26	22	2	2	9	100
		18			69			13		

Table 5.6 Inter-relationship among age, caste and education of respondents of Bulandshahr district

Educational level	Age-group (years) 20-35			36-50			51-65			Total
	SC	OBC	UC	SC	OBC	UC	SC	OBC	UC	
Uneducated	4	2	-	5	7	-	3	2	3	26
Up to Primary	-	3	1	6	11	18	1	4	11	55
Up to Secondary	-	2	-	-	11	2	-	1	1	17
Above Secondary	-	-	-	-	1	1	-	-	-	2
Total	4	7	1	11	30	21	4	7	15	100
		12			62			26		

Inter-relationship among caste, income and education variables

The inter-relationship among cast, income and education of respondents of Rampur district reveals that 23.08 per cent OBC respondents were having education up to primary level earning less than Rs. 1000 per annum whereas their counterparts of Bulandshahr district were only 11.36 per cent (Table 5.8).

Occupation

Table 5.9 reveals that cent per cent respondents of Rampur district were having farming as main occupation whereas only 94 per cent respondents of Bulandshahr were having farming as main occupation. It indicates that six respondents which have main occupation either service or business were having farming as secondary occupation.

Martial status

Of the 200 selected respondents, for the study all but nine respondents were married (Table 5.10). Only one respondent was unmarried at the time of interview and five were widows and three were divorces.

Table 5.7 Inter-relationship among caste, income and education of respondents of Rampur district

Educational level	Income-group (years) Below 1000			1000-1500			More 1500			Total
	SC	OBC	UC	SC	OBC	UC	SC	OBC	UC	
Uneducated	7	6	1	3	5	13	2	1	-	38
Up to Primary	2	9	2	10	5	6	-	2	1	37
Up to Secondary	-	1	4	6	7	-	19			
Above Secondary	-	1	-	4	1	-	6			
Total	9	16	5	17	20	27	2	3	1	100
		30			64			6		

Table 5.8 Inter-relationship among caste, income and education of respondents of Bulandshahr district

Educational level	Income-group (years) Below 1000			1000-1500			More 1500			Total
	SC	OBC	UC	SC	OBC	UC	SC	OBC	UC	
Uneducated	5	3	3	8	6	1	-	-	-	26
Up to Primary	1	5	11	3	23	9	2	1	-	55
Up to Secondary	-	6	4	-	-	7	-	-	-	17
Above Secondary	-	-	-	-	-	2	-	-	-	2
Total	6	14	18	11	29	19	2	1	-	100
		38			59			3		

Table 5.9 Occupation-wise distribution of respondents

Occupation	Rampur		Bulandshahr		Pooled	
	Main	Secondary	Main	Secondary	Main	Secondary
Farming	100	-	94	6	194	6
Caste occupation	-	9	-	13	-	22
Service	-	-	2	18	2	18
Business	-	29	4	-	4	29
Total	100	38	100	37	200	75

Table 5.10 Martial status of respondents

Income group (Rs.)	Rampur		Bulandshahr		Pooled	
	F	%	F	%	F	%
Unmarried	1	1.00	-	-	1	0.50
Married	96	96.00	95	95.00	191	95.50
Widow/Divorcee	3	3.00	5	5.00	8	4.00
Total	100	100.00	100	100.00	200	100.00

Social participation

The perusal of Table 5.11 reveals that 62 per cent respondents have no participation in any social organisation whereas 23.50 per cent respondents were members of one social organisation. This clearly points out the fact that rural women, generally, do not take part in social activities and keep themselves away from social institutions.

Inter-relationship among income, education and social participation

The inter-relationship among income, education and social participation of respondents of Rampur district reveals that 83.33 per cent respondents having income more than Rs. 1500 p.a.,

45.31 per cent respondents having income below Rs. 1000 were participating in social activities (Table 5.12). It shows that as the income increases the social participation also enhanced. Similar trend has been observed from Table 5.13 which shows that all the three respondents earning more than Rs. 1500 p.a. were participating in social institutions. Varma (1989) has also stated that respondents of higher socio-economic status participate more in comparison to respondents of medium and low socio-economic status.

Table 5.11 Social participation of respondents

Social participation	Rampur		Bulandshahr		Pooled	
	F	%	F	%	F	%
No membership	56	56.00	68	68.00	124	62.00
Member of one organization	28	28.00	19	19.00	47	23.50
Member of more than one organization	16	16.00	13	13.00	29	14.50
Total	100	100.00	100	100.00	200	100.00

Family profile

Family type

It is evident from Table 5.14 that joint family system in rural areas is disintegrating into nuclear families. Though, joint family system has its own advantages but now-a-days most of the families prefer to live independently. There were 67.50 per cent of total households under study were having nuclear families. About 64 per cent and 71 per cent were nuclear families to which respondents of Rampur and Bulandshahr districts, respectively belonged. The findings are in conformity with the findings of Singh et al. (1968) and Yadav (1986).

Table 5.12 Inter-relationship among income, education and social participation of respondents of Rampur district

Educational level	Income group (Rs.) Below 1000			1000-1500			Above 1500			Total
	A	B	C	A	B	C	A	B	C	
Uneducated	6	-	-	14	12	6	-	-	-	38
Up top Primary	91	4	15	5	1	1	1	-	37	
Up to Secondary	5	3	2	2	3	2	-	2	-	19
Above Secondary	-	-	-	4	-	-	-	1	1	6
Total	20	4	6	35	20	9	1	4	1	100
		30			64			6		

A = No membership;
B = Member of one organization
C = Member of more than one organization.

Table 5.13 Inter-relationship among income, education and social participation of respondents of Bulandshahr district

Educational level	Income group (Rs.) Below 1000			1000-1500			Above 1500			Total
	A	B	C	A	B	C	A	B	C	
Uneducated	71	-	13	5	-	-	-	-	26	
Up to Primary	11	4	1	29	2	8	-	-	-	55
Up to Secondary	8	3	3	-	2	-	-	1	-	17
Above Secondary	-	-	-	-	-	-	-	1	1	2
Total	26	8	4	42	9	8	-	2	1	100
		38			59			3		

Table 5.14 Distribution of respondents according to type of family

Type of family	Rampur		Bulandshahr		Pooled	
	F	%	F	%	F	%
Joint	36	36.00	29	29.00	65	32.50
Nuclear	64	64.00	71	71.00	135	67.50
Total	100	100.00	100	100.00	200	100.00

Family-size

The small family norm as propagated by the government has not been able to get adopted by rural mass because of extensive labour force is demanded for meeting needs of farming. This phenomenon can be seen from the perusal of Table 5.15 which shows that 41.50 per cent families have more than five members and 58.50 per cent families have less than five members.

Table 5.15 Family-size of respondents

Type of family	Rampur		Bulandshahr		Pooled	
	F	%	F	%	F	%
< 5 members	63	63.00	54	54.00	117	58.50
> 5 members	37	37.00	46	46.00	83	41.50
Total	100	100.00	100	100.00	200	100.00

Family education

Education of all the members of family is important for enhancing knowledge and adoption of improved farm and technologies. It may be seen from Table 5.16 that 64 per cent of total families have low educational status and only 7.50 per cent families have higher educational status. It was also observed that low income group families did not encourage their children for acquiring education because of their children were engaged in other work. Varma (1989) has also observed the similar phenomenon.

Table 5.16 Family's educational status

Educational status	Rampur		Bulandshahr		Pooled	
	F	%	F	%	F	%
Low	55	55.00	73	73.00	128	64.00
Medium	36	36.00	21	21.00	57	28.50
High	9	9.00	6	6.00	15	7.50
Total	100	100.00	100	100.00	200	100.00

House type

It was observed that 55.50 per cent of respondents resided in mixed type of houses which have approximate average value Rs. 79,788.30 (Table 5.17). It was also observed that, generally, katcha houses were owned by families having low income but some of them also owned mixed houses. Pucca houses were, generally, owned by medium and high income groups families.

Family income

The annual income of 51.50 per cent families was below Rs. 50,000 and of 15 per cent families above Rs. One lakh (Table 5.18). The average annual income of 51.50 per cent families was Rs. 38, 761.00, of 33 per cent families was Rs. 87,837.00 and of 15 per cent families was Rs. 1,03,860.00. The overall average income was Rs. 64, 966.31 p.a. This shows that the families of respondents were not very financially sound.

Land holding

Table 5.19 reveals that 82 per cent households were having land for cultivation whereas 18 per cent households have no land. The average size of land holding of the marginal category households was 0.436 ha, small category 1.461 ha and of large category 2.864 ha.

Table 5.17 Distribution of respondents according to type of houses

Type of House	Rampur			Bulandshahr			Pooled		
	Frequency	Per cent	Av. Cost (Rs)	Frequency	Per cent	Av. Cost (Rs)	Frequency	Per cent	Av. Cost (Rs)
Katcha	21	21.00	4567.00	27	27.0	5130.00	48	24.00	4883.69
Mixed	51	51.00	75171.00	60	60.0	83713.00	111	55.50	79788.30
Pucca	28	28.00	158311.00	13	13.0	181151.00	41	20.50	165552.95
Total	100	100.00	-	100	100.00	-	200	100.00	-

Table 5.18 Distribution of households according to annual income

Income group (Rs.)	Rampur		Bulandshahr		Pooled	
	F	%	F	%	F	%
Below 50,000	55	55.00	48	48.00	103	51.50
50,000-1,00,000	32	32.00	35	35.00	67	33.00
Above 1,00,000	13	13.00	17	17.00	30	15.00
Total	100	100.00	100	100.00	200	100.00

Table 5.19 Land holding-wise distribution of households

Category	Rampur		Bulandshahr		Pooled	
	F	%	F	%	F	%
Landless	16	16.00	20	20.00	36	18.00
Marginal	43	43.00	39	39.00	82	41.00
Small	18	18.00	24	24.00	42	21.00
Large	23	23.00	17	17.00	40	20.00
Total	100	100.00	100	100.00	200	100.00

Farm power

It was observed that 40.86 per cent households possessed 1-2 draught animals, 29.27 per cent households possessed 3-4 draught animals and 17.68 per cent households possessed above draught animals (Table 5.20). Only 12.19 per cent households possessed tractors for cultivation. These households fall in the category of small and large holdings.

Milch animals

Table 5.21 reveals that 44 per cent and 33 per cent households of Rampur and Bulandshahr districts, respectively were possessing 2-4 milch animals. Only 9.50 per cent of total 200 households possessed above 6 milch animals. These households belonged to large income group because they can only afford to feed and care them. The average value per milch animal came to Rs. 11,761.00.

Table 5.20 Distribution of households according to possession of farm power

Farm power	Rampur		Bulandshahr		Pooled	
	F	%	F	%	F	%
Tractors	12	14.29	8	10.00	20	12.19
Draught animals						
Up to 2	37	44.05	30	37.50	67	40.86
3-4	19	22.62	29	36.25	48	29.27
Above 4	16	19.04	13	16.25	29	17.68
Total	84	100.00	80	100.00	164	100.00

Table 5.21 Distribution of households according to possession of milch animals

Milch animal (No.)	Rampur		Bulandshahr		Pooled	
	F	%	F	%	F	%
1-2	39	39.00	41	41.00	80	40.00
2-4	44	44.00	33	33.00	77	38.50
4-6	10	10.00	14	14.00	24	12.00
Above 6	7	7.00	12	12.00	19	9.50
Total	100	100.00	100	100.00	200	100.00

Materials possession

Now-a-days, possession of modern household appliances and gadgets decide the standard of living. Very family likes to have costlier items for house, be it operated or not is the other thing. Table 5.22 reveals this fact because fifty per cent households of the study areas possessed between 10-25 items of all categories i.e. less and high prestigious. The average value of possessed materials for high income group families was Rs. 21,363.00, and for medium income group families was Rs. 13,836.00 and for low-income group families was Rs. 8954.00. It was observed that transistors sets, television and pressure cooker have found place in almost all the households.

Table 5.22 Distribution of households according to materials possession

Material possession (No.)	Rampur		Bulandshahr		Pooled	
	F	%	F	%	F	%
1-10	14	14.00	23	23.00	37	18.50
10-25	57	57.00	43	43.00	100	50.00
Above 25	29	29.00	34	34.00	63	31.50
Total	100	100.00	100	100.00	200	100.00

Possession of agricultural implements

It was observed that 78.66 per cent households were possessing agricultural implements up to four numbers. Out of 12.19 per cent tractor owner households, only 4.88 per cent were possessing tractor driven agricultural implements (Table 5.23). These households belonged to high income group.

Table 5.23 Distribution of households according to possession of agricultural implements

Agricultural implements (No.)	Rampur		Bulandshahr		Pooled	
	F	%	F	%	F	%
Up to 4	61	72.62	68	85.00	129	78.66
4 and above	18	21.43	9	11.25	27	16.46
Tractor driven implements	5	5.95	3	3.75	8	4.88
Total	84	100.00	80	100.00	164	100.00

KNOWLEDGE AND ADOPTION OF TECHNOLOGIES

Transfer of technology is a process by which innovations are exchanged between individuals and organizations that are involved in research and development, on the one hand and in putting technological innovations into use on the other. It does not mean adopting new idea, procedure or product just by transferring physically. Mere physical shift will not ensure its use. Since people have their attitudes, opinions and values, new technology has to work within the social environment, thus, the technology must be compatible with social and cultural systems both.

Adoption of technology depends on knowledge of and interest in technology. Without knowledge and interest, adoption of technology will suffer. Hence, it was found essential to study the knowledge, interest and adaptation of technologies by the respondents of the study area.

Knowledge level of technologies

Farm technologies

Crop-wise participation of the respondents of both the districts is presented in Table 5.24. It was observed that 61 respondents of Rampur district were participating in wheat, 65 in paddy and 43 in sugarcane cultivation whereas in Bulandshahr district, 58 respondents were participating in wheat, 62 in paddy and 39 in sugarcane cultivation. Wheat and paddy are the main crops of Rabi and Kharif seasons in both the districts. Though, maize crop is sown in large area in Rampur but its productivity is less than paddy, therefore more people adopt paddy cultivation instead maize. In Bulandshahr, maize is sown in small area in comparison to other crops of Kharif season. Sugarcane, the cash crop, is grown in large area in both the districts as its productivity is quite high.

(a) Wheat crop technologies

education-wise distribution of respondents having knowledge of technologies of wheat, paddy and sugarcane crops was analysed. Table 5.25 reveals that, in Rampur district, 65.57 per cent respondents have knowledge of fertilizers and its application in wheat cultivation. Of this, 47.50 per cent of respondents having knowledge were educated up to primary level and 35 per cent respondents were uneducated. It was also observed that two respondents who were graduates did not know about fertilizer's appropriate dose to be used and Plant protection measures for controlling diseases and pests. The reason of this having no knowledge was their non-participation in application of these activities. Among the uneducated respondents, 70.37 and 62.96 per cent (vertical) respondents were having knowledge about technologies used in sowing and intercultural operation, respectively.

Table 5.24 Crop-wise participation of respondents

Crop-group	Rampur	Bulandshahr	Pooled
Wheat	19	17	36
Paddy	17	23	40
Sugarcane	4	12	16
Wheat + Paddy	30	32	62
Wheat + Sugarcane	21	20	41
Paddy + Sugarcane	27	18	45
Wheat + Paddy + Sugarcane	9	11	20

(Respondents participated in cultivation of other crops also along with the above crop-groups).

In Bulandshahr district, 65.52 per cent respondents were having knowledge of technologies related with Intercultural operations and 55.17 per cent respondents were having knowledge about fertilizers and its application in wheat cultivation. It was observed that 77.27 per cent respondents of both the districts having knowledge of fertilizers and intercultural technologies were educated up to primary level (Table 5.26).

(b) Paddy crop technologies

The perusal of Table 5.27 shows that 72.31 per cent respondents of Rampur district were having knowledge of transplantation technology. Of this, 48.94 per cent respondents having knowledge of this technology were uneducated, and

Table 5.25. Respondents having knowledge of technologies of wheat cultivation

(Number)

Technology	Rampur					Bulandshahr				
	Uneducated (n_1=27)	Up to Primary (n_2=23)	Up to Secondary (n_3=9)	Above Secondary (n_4=2)	Total (N=61)	Uneducated (n_1 = 24)	Up to Primary (n_2=21)	Up to Secondary (n_3=13)	Above Secondary	Total (N=58)
HYV	11 (39.29)	9 (32.14)	7 (25.00)	1 (3.57)	28 (45.90)*	13 (43.33)	11 (34.67)	6 (20.00)	-	30 (51.72)*
Sowing	19 (51.35)	13 (35.13)	3 (8.11)	2 (5.41)	37 (60.66)	15 (40.54)	17 (45.95)	5 (13.51)	-	37 (63.79)
Intercultural operations	17 (43.59)	15 (38.46)	6 (15.38)	1 (2.57)	39 (63.93)	11 (28.95)	19 (50.00)	8 (21.05)	-	38 (65.52)
Fertilizers and its application	14 (35.00)	19 (47.50)	7 (17.50)	- (65.57)	40 (28.12)	9 (46.68)	15 (25.00)	8 (55.17)	-	32
Plant protection Measures	10 (34.48)	14 (48.28)	5 (17.24)	- (47.54)	29 (31.82)	7 (40.91)	9 (27.27)	6 (37.93)	-	22

(Figures in parentheses are horizontal percentages and asterisk marked in total; column are vertical percentages)

36.17 per cent respondents were educated up to primary level. It means 71.43 per cent of total respondents who were not well educated having knowledge of transplantation technology whereas 77.78 per cent of total respondents passed secondary and above secondary having knowledge of this technology. It was also observed that 67.69 per cent respondents were having knowledge of seed bed preparation technology. Of this, 47.73 per cent respondents were uneducated and 43.18 per cent respondents were educated up to primary level.

Table 5.26 Respondents (pooled) having knowledge of technologies of wheat cultivation

Technology	Number of respondents				
	Uneducated (n1=51) (n2 = 44)	Up to Primary (n3 = 22)	Up to Secondary (n4 =2)	Above Secondary	Total (N = 119)
HYV	24 (41.38)	20 (34.48)	13 (22.42)	1 (1.72)	58 (48.74)*
Sowing	34 (45.95)	30 (40.54)	8 (10.81)	2 (2.70)	74 (62.18)
Intercultural Operations	28 (36.36)	34 (44.16)	14 (18.18)	1 (1.30)	77 (64.71)
Fertilizers & its application	23 (31.94)	34 (47.22)	15 (20.84)	-	72 (60.50)
Plant protection measures	17 (33.33)	23 (45.10)	11 (21.57)	-	51 (42.86)

(Figures in parentheses are horizontal percentages and asterisk marked in total column are vertical percentages).

In Bulandshahr district too, large number of respondents (72.58 per cent) were having knowledge of transplantation technology. Of this, 46.67 per cent respondents were uneducated and 42.22 per cent educated up to primary level. It was observed that like their counterparts of Rampur district high percentage of respondents educated up to primary level were having knowledge of paddy cultivation technologies.

Analysis of pooled data (Table 5.28) reveals that 72.44, 67.72 and 51.18 per cent respondents were having knowledge of transplantation, nursery raising and fertilizers application technology, respectively.

Table 5.27. Respondents having knowledge of technologies of paddy cultivation

(Number)

Technology	Rampur					Bulandshahr				
	Uneducated (n_1=30)	Up to Primary (n_2=26)	Up to Secondary (n_3=6)	Above Secondary (n_4=3)	Total (N=65)	Uneducated (n_1 = 24)	Up to Primary (n_2=31)	Up to Secondary (n_3=5)	Above Secondary (n_4=3)	Total (N=62)
HYV	7	9	3	2	21	4	9	2	1	16
	(33.33)	(42.86)	(14.29)	(9.52)	(32.31)*	(25.00)	(56.25)	(12.50)	(6.25)	(25.81)*
Seed bed	21	19	4	-	44	9	13	4	2	28
Preparation	(47.13)	(43.18)	(9.09)	(67.69)	(32.14)	(46.43)	(14.29)	(7.14)	(45.16)*	
Time of nursery	19	16	5	2	42	17	21	4	2	44
Raising	(45.24)	(38.10)	(11.90)	(4.76)	(64.61)	(38.64)	(47.73)	(9.09)	(4.54)	(70.97)
Transplantation	23	17	5	2	47	21	19	3	2	45
	(48.94)	(36.17)	(10.64)	(4.25)	(72.31)	(46.67)	(42.22)	(6.67)	(4.44)	(72.58)
Fertilizers and its	14	11	3	2	30	16	13	4	2	35
application	(46.67)	(36.67)	(10.00)	(6.66)	(46.15)	(45.71)	(37.15)	(11.43)	(5.71)	(56.45)
Plant protection	12	10	2	2	26	6	5	2	1	14
measures	(46.16)	(38.46)	(7.69)	(40.00)	(42.86)	(35.71)	(14.29)	(7.14)	(22.58)	
Intercultural	10	11	3	1	25	6	7	3	1	17
operations	(40.00)	(44.00)	(12.00)	(4.00)	(38.46)	(35.29)	(41.18)	(17.65)	(5.88)	(22.42)

(Figures in parentheses are horizontal percentages and asterisk marked in total column are vertical percentages)

Table 5.28 Respondents (pooled) having knowledge of technologies of paddy cultivation

Technology	Number of respondents				
	Uneducated (n_1=54)	Up to Primary (n_2 = 57)	Up to Secondary (n_3 = 11)	Above Secondary (n_4 =5)	Total (N = 127)
HYV	11 (29.73)	18 (48.65)	5 (13.51)	3 (8.11)	37 (29.13)*
Seed bed Preparation	30 (41.67)	32 (44.44)	8 (11.11)	2 (2.78)	72 (56.69)
Time of nursery Raising	36 (41.86)	37 (43.03)	9 (10.47)	4 (4.65)	86 (67.72)
Transplantation	44 (47.83)	36 (39.13)	8 (8.69)	4 (4.35)	92 (72.44)
Fertilizers and its application	30 (46.15)	24 (36.92)	7 (10.77)	4 (6.16)	65 (51.18)
Plant protection measures	18 (45.00)	15 (37.50)	4 (10.00)	3 (7.50)	40 (31.50)
Intercultural operations	16 (38.09)	18 (42.86)	6 (14.29)	2 (4.76)	42 (33.07)

(Figures in parentheses are horizontal percentages and asterisk marked in total column are vertical percentages).

(c) Sugarcane crop technologies

In sugarcane cultivation, of the 43 respondents of Rampur district, 26 respondents were uneducated, 12 respondents were uneducated, 12 respondents were educated up to primary level and only 5 respondents were educated up to secondary level. About 76.74 per cent respondents were having knowledge of intercultural operations related technology. Of this, 51.52 per cent respondents were uneducated and 33.33 per cent respondents were educated up to primary level (Table 5.29). The table also revealed that only 37.21 per cent respondents were having knowledge of HYV technology.

In Bulandshahr district, 74.36 per cent respondents were having knowledge of technology related with intercultural operations. Of this 48.28 per cent respondents were uneducated and 24.14 per cent respondents were educated up to secondary level.

Analysis of pooled data (Table 5.30) also shows that the largest number of respondents (75.61 per cent) were having knowledge of technology related with intercultural operations and only 42.68 per cent respondents were having knowledge of technology of improved varieties.

Knowledge level

For assessment of knowledge level of respondents, one score was allotted to every affirmative and correct response. Total scores obtained by each respondent for wheat, paddy and sugarcane crops, respectively, were categorised. Association of respondents educational level and their knowledge level was calculated and presented in Tables 5.31, 5.32 and 5.33.

Table 5.31 reveals that uneducated and primary educated respondents of Bulandshahr district have more knowledge (av. Score) of wheat cultivation technologies than their counterparts of Rampur district but, contrary to this, respondents of Rampur district educated up to secondary level have more knowledge (av. Score 12.00). Pooled data reveal that uneducated respondents have average score 7.37, up to primary level educated 7.12 and up to secondary level educated 10.58. This shows that there is no difference in the average scores of uneducated and primary educated respondents.

In case of knowledge of paddy cultivation technologies, the respondents of Bulandshahr district have more knowledge than their counterparts of Rampur district. The average scores of uneducated, up to primary and secondary level educated respondents of Bulandshahr district were 9.08, 9.16 and 8.20, respectively, which are greater than average scores obtained by respondents of Rampur district. Pooled data analysis showed that up to primary level educated respondents has more knowledge than uneducated and up to secondary level educated respondents.

Table 5.29. Respondents having knowledge of technologies of sugarcane cultivation

(Number)

Technology	Rampur					Bulandshahr				
	Uneducated (n_1=26)	Up to Primary (n_2=12)	Up to Secondary (n_3=5)	Above Secondary	Total (N=43)	Uneducated (n_1 = 22)	Up to Primary (n_2=8)	Up to Secondary (n_3=7)	Above Secondary (n_4=2)	Total (N=39)
HYV	5	7	4	-	16	7	6	4	2	19
	(31.25)	(43.75)	(25.00)		(37.21)*	(36.84)	(31.58)	(21.05)	(10.53)	(48.71)
Seed rate	13	6	3	-	22	9	5	5	2	21
	(59.09)	(27.27)	(13.64)		(51.16)	(42.86)	(23.81)	(23.81)	(9.52)	(53.85)
Seed	11	8	4	-	23	9	6	5	2	22
Treatment(47.83)	(34.78)	(17.39)	(53.49)		(40.91)	(27.27)	(22.73)	(9.09)	(56.41)	
Intercultural	17	11	5	-	33	14	6	7	2	29
Operations	(51.52)	(33.33)	(15.15)		(76.74)	(48.28)	(20.69)	(24.14)	(6.89)	(74.36)
Fertilizers and its	14	9	4	-	27	10	7	5	2	24
Application	(51.85)	(33.33)	(14.82)		(62.79)	(41.67)	(29.17)	(20.83)	(8.33)	(61.54)
Plant protection	8	7	5	-	20	6	4	3	1	14
Measures	(40.00)	(35.00)	(25.00)		(46.51)	(42.86)	(28.57)	(21.43)	(7.14)	(35.90)

(Figures in parentheses are horizontal percentages and asterisk marked in total column are vertical percentages)

Table 5.30 Respondents (pooled) having knowledge of technologies of sugarcane cultivation

Technology	Number of respondents				
	Uneducated (n_1 = 48)	Up to Primary (n_2 – 20)	Up to Secondary (n_3 = 12)	Above Secondary (n_4 = 2)	Total (N = 82)
HYV	12 (34.29)	13 (37.14)	8 (22.86)	2 (5.71)	35 (42.68)
Seed rate	22 (51.16)	11 (25.58)	8 (18.60)	2 (4.66)	43 (52.44)
Seed treatment	20 (44.44)	14 (31.11)	9 (20.00)	2 (4.45)	45 (54.88)
Fertilizers and its application	24 (47.06)	16 (31.37)	9 (17.65)	2 (3.92)	51 (62.19)
Plant protection measures	14 (41.18)	11 (32.35)	8 (23.53)	1 (2.94)	34 (41.46)
Intercultural operations	31 (50.00)	17 (27.42)	12 (19.35)	2 (3.23)	62 (75.61)

(Figures in parentheses are horizontal percentages and asterisk marked in total column are vertical percentages)

Table 5.33 reveals that 72.09 per cent of total respondents engaged in sugarcane cultivation in Rampur district were having poor knowledge. The average scores varied between 5.34 and 6.99. In Bulandshahr district, 56.41 per cent respondents were having fair knowledge of sugarcane cultivation technologies. Pooled data analysis showed that 58.54 per cent respondents have poor knowledge and 40.24 per cent have fair knowledge. Only one respondent who was uneducated was having good knowledge.

Non-significant Chi-square values show that there is no association between respondents educational level and their knowledge about technologies of wheat, paddy and sugarcane crops. It means whatever knowledge respondents were having of these technologies were gained through their work experience. Varma (1989) has also reported that although women were so much involved in farming but they do not hold

Table 5.31 Association of educational and knowledge level of wheat cultivation technologies

(Number)

Educational level	Rampur ($n_1 = 61$)				Bulandshahr ($n_2 = 58$)				Pooled (N = 119)			
	Poor	Fair	Good	± S.D.	Poor	Fair	Good	± S.D.	Poor	Fair	Good	± S.D.
Uneducated	16	10	1	6.67 ± 3.04	12	10	2	8.17 ± 3.90	28	20	3	7.37 ± 3.53
Upto Primary	13	7	3	6.49 ± 3.30	13	7	1	7.81 ± 3.01	26	14	4	7.12 ± 3.17
Upto Secondary	2	4	3	12.0 ± 4.56	6	7	-	9.61 ± 3.80	8	11	3	10.58 ± 3.94
Above Secondary	-	1	1	12.80 ± 4.95	-	-	-	-	-	1	-	12.00 ± 4.95
c^2 - value	1.381 (P > 0.05)				0.999 (P > 0.05)				4.403 (P > 0.05)			

Table 5.32 Association of educational and knowledge level of paddy cultivation technologies

(Number)

Educational level	Rampur (n_1 = 65)				Bulandshahr (n_2 = 52)				Pooled (N = 127)			
	Poor	Fair	Good	± S.D.	Poor	Fair	Good	± S.D.	Poor	Fair	Good	± S.D.
Uneducated	18	9	3	6.50 ± 3.42	9	14	1	9.08 ± 3.51	27	23	4	7.64 ± 3.13
Upto Primary	16	8	2	7.69 ± 3.80	16	12	3	9.16 ± 3.96	32	20	5	8.49 ± 3.17
Upto Secondary	4	1	1	7.58 ± 3.32	3	2	-	8.20 ± 4.32	7	3	1	7.87 ± 3.98
Above Secondary	2	1	-	9.16 ± 2.51	-	2	-	9.00 ± 1.41	2	3	-	9.10 ± 1.93
c^2 - value	0.056 (P > 0.05)				0.928 (P > 0.05)				0.472 (P > 0.05)			

Table 5.33 Association of educational and knowledge level of sugarcane cultivation technologies

(Number)

Educational level	Rampur (n_1 = 43)				Bulandshahr (n_2 = 39)				Pooled (N = 82)			
	Poor	Fair	Good	± S.D.	Poor	Fair	Good	± S.D.	Poor	Fair	Good	± S.D.
Uneducated	19	6	1	5.34 ± 3.16	9	13	-	6.13 ± 3.09	28	19	1	5.70 ± 3.08
Upto Primary	9	3	-	6.83 ± 2.61	5	3	-	6.61 ± 3.17	14	6	-	6.74 ± 3.01
Upto Secondary	3	2	-	6.99 ± 3.61	3	4	-	8.87 ± 3.81	6	6	-	8.09 ± 3.59
Above Secondary	-	-	-	-	-	2	-	10.50 ± 2.12	-	2	-	10.50 ± 2.12
c^2 - value	0.032 (P > 0.05)				0.149 (P > 0.05)				2.513 (P > 0.05)			

adequate knowledge of modern crop cultivation technologies. Whatever they have learnt, it is by way of their involvement in farming. There had been no deliberate attempt made to give them education about the modern technologies. Gurusamy (1987) and Sankaran and Perumal (1999) have found that level of knowledge was high in big farm women as compared to small farm women category. This is due to better level of education, farming experience, mass media exposure, etc.

(ii) Animal husbandry technologies

Table 5.34 reveals that almost equal percentage of respondents were having fair knowledge of animal husbandry technologies in Rampur and Bulandshahr districts. Only 15 per cent of total respondents were having good knowledge and, of this, 43.33 per cent respondents were educated up to primary level. The table also shows that in spite of increase in average score with the enhancement of educational level, no significant association was observed. All the Chi-square values are found to be non-significant. This indicates that education has certainly enhanced their knowledge of animal husbandry technologies but not to that level which is required off from these respondents. Tripathi (1991) has observed that rural women have significantly higher level of knowledge about all the technologies except the cultivation of nutritious fodder. Jamal (1989) has observed that farm women need to be equipped with practical knowledge in feeding, management and milk products making.

(iii) Household technologies

The improved household technologies are the devices used at home for efficient working which are considerable time and labour saving. The improved household technologies covered under the study are energy saving devices like smokeless chulha, solar cooker, bio-gas and LPG burners, labour saving devices like bal-bearing *chakki*, rice mill, washing machine, storage bins, etc. total seventeen gadgets and appliances were included for the study. Respondents were asked about brand of the appliance/gadget, availability from the organization, raw materials used, functioning, etc. the correct response was assigned one score and total scores were then categorised in three categories as poor, fair and good knowledge.

Table 5.34 Association of educational and knowledge level of animal husbandry technologies

(Number)

Educational level	Rampur				Bulandshahr				Pooled			
	Poor	Fair	Good	± S.D.	Poor	Fair	Good	± S.D.	Poor	Fair	Good	± S.D.
Uneducated	11	23	4	9.92 ± 3.57	9	12	5	10.46 ± 4.10	20	35	0	10.14 ± 3.49
Upto Primary	8	24	5	10.45 ± 3.52	10	37	8	10.76 ± 3.36	18	61	13	10.63 ± 3.39
Upto Secondary	2	11	6	12.42 ± 3.73	3	13	1	10.17 ± 2.63	5	24	7	11.35 ± 3.11
Above Secondary	-	5	1	14.0 ± 3.58	-	2	-	17.50 ± 2.12	-	7	1	14.87 ± 2.94
c^2 - value	2.33 (P > 0.05)				3.26 (P > 0.05)				5.36 (P > 0.05)			

Pooled data (Table 5.35) reveal that 28.5 per cent respondents were having poor knowledge. This indicated that almost half of the total respondents have fair knowledge. Table also shows that knowledge level is directly associated with educational level of respondents since all the Chi-square values are significant.

Of the eight above secondary educated respondents, six were having good knowledge level and two fair levels. These respondents have acquired information and technical know-how of appliances and gadgets from mass media available to them and through relatives and friends. Kaur and Sharma (1991) have also reported that level of exposure of the respondents to information sources, education of the respondent, highest education in the family and income of the family were significantly and highly associated with knowledge about improved household technology.

(B) Interest in technologies

(i) Farm technologies

Interest of respondents in modern farm technologies was assessed on three continuum scale and average score was obtained for each technology. The results presented in Table 5.36 are showing interest of respondents in modern farm technologies of wheat cultivation. It is evident from the table that respondent shave shown the highest interest in fertilizers and manures. Next in preponderance were irrigation, plant protection measures and improved varieties. The average scores ranged between 0.613 to 0.235. The respondents of Rampur and Bulandshahr districts have assigned 4th rank to improved varieties. This shows that they were least interested in use of improved varieties. The respondents of Bulandshahr district were most interested in irrigation technology. Their interest in their technology was no account of their views that use of irrigation might enhance productivity. It was also observed that no significant variations were existing in interest levels between districts as well as technologies.

Table 5.35 Association of educational and knowledge level of household technologies

(Number)

Educational level	Rampur				Bulandshahr				Pooled			
	Poor	Fair	Good	± S.D.	Poor	Fair	Good	± S.D.	Poor	Fair	Good	± S.D.
Uneducated	18	11	9	9.36 ± 2.61	14	9	3	8.87 ± 2.11	32	20	12	9.16 ± 2.73
Upto Primary	6	20	11	10.85 ± 3.11	9	27	19	9.63 ± 2.18	15	47	30	10.12 ± 3.13
Upto Secondary	5	6	8	11.10 ± 3.21	5	7	5	10.76 ± 3.53	10	13	13	10.94 ± 3.39
Above Secondary	-	2	4	16.25 ± 3.93	-	-	2	18.50 ± 2.12	-	2	6	16.81 ± 3.17
c^2 - value	13.54 (P > 0.01)				13.97 (P > 0.01)				23.32 (P > 0.01)			

Table 5.36 Respondents showing interest in wheat cultivation technologies

Technology	Rampur		Bulandshahr		Pooled	
	Av. score	Rank	Av. Score	Rank	Av. Score	Rank
HYV	0.115	IV	0.362	IV	O.235	IV
Irrigation	0.590	II	0.569	I	0.580	II
Fertilizers and Manures	0.672	I	0.552	II	0.613	I
Plant protection Measures	0.377	III	0.500	III	0.437	III
F-value for District Technologies					4.46 (P> 0.05)	
Spearman's rank Correlation					0.80 (P< 0.01)	

Table 5.37 Respondents showing interest in paddy cultivation technologies

Technology	Rampur		Bulandshahr		Pooled	
	Av. score	Rank	Av. Score	Rank	Av. Score	Rank
HYV	0.231	III	0.242	III	0.236	III
Nursery bed raising	0.446	II	0.290	II	0.370	II
Irrigation	0.077	V	0.113	V	0.094	V
Fertilizers and Manures	0.492	I	0.387	I	0.441	I
Plant protection Manures	0.169	IV	0.210	IV	0.189	IV
F-value for Districts Technologies				9.37 (P> 0.05)		

The perusal of Table 5.37 shows that, like wheat, in paddy cultivation, respondents have assigned first rank to Fertilizers and manures. This indicates that respondents were highly interested in application of Fertilizers and manures so that paddy yield might increase. They have given second rank to nursery bed raising and third rank to improved varieties. They have less interest in Plant protection measures and irrigation.

It is clear from the Table 5.38 that respondents have shown the highest liking for improved varieties of sugarcane by assigning the first rank. Next to this, their liking was for irrigation and plant protection measures. In their view improved varieties are best suited for enhancing productivity of sugarcane. Table 5.38 also shows significant variations in the interest shown to the sugarcane cultivation Technologies.

Table 5.38 Respondents showing interest in sugarcane cultivation technologies

Technology	Rampur		Bulandshahr		Pooled	
	Av. score	Rank	Av. Score	Rank	Av. Score	Rank
HYV	0.814	I	0.667	I	0.743	I
Irrigation	0.442	II	0.538	II	0.488	II
Fertilizers and Manures	0.419	III	0.308	V	0.366	IV
Plant protection measures	0.372	IV	0.436	III	0.402	III
Dislodging	0.302	V	0.333	IV	0.317	V
Earthing	0.116	VI	0.179	VI	0.146	VI
F-value for Districts Technologies					14.96 (P< 0.001)	
Spearman's rank Correlation					0.83 (P< 0.001)	

(ii) Animal husbandry technologies

Like farm technologies, interest in animal husbandry technologies was also assessed through the same procedure. The results presented in Table 5.39 shows that respondents have shown the highest interest in milk products preparation technology. Next to this, they were interested in use of dung for domestic and marketing purpose. They were least interested in breeding technology. They were of the view that it is of the male domain and they have nothing to do with this technology. Though, they realised that efficient improved breeding technology would enhance milk production, but still they were not more interested in this technology.

Table 5.39 Respondents showing interest in animal husbandry technologies

Technology	Rampur		Bulandshahr		Pooled	
	Av. score	Rank	Av. Score	Rank	Av. Score	Rank
Breeding	0.10	VIII	0.13	VIII	0.11	VIII
Feeding	0.65	III	0.71	III	0.68	III
Fodder growing	0.49	V	0.59	V	0.54	V
Vaccination	0.38	VI	0.26	VII	0.32	VII
Treating sick Animals	0.33	VII	0.37	VI	0.35	VI
Use of dung	0.87	I	0.82	II	0.84	II
Preparation of milk Products	0.84	II	0.88	I	0.86	I
Marketing	0.56	IV	0.62	IV	0.59	IV
F-value for Districts Technologies					55.16 (P< 0.001)	
Spearman's rank correlation					0.95(P< 0.001)	

Their interest in technologies varied significantly but no significant variations were observed in the interest shown in two districts. This shows the pattern of showing interest is almost similar in both the districts.

(iii) Household technologies

It is evident from Table 5.40 that respondents of both the district have shown the highest interest in grain storage technology. During interview, respondents have not only shown their interest in improved grain storage technology but also they were having high knowledge about EDB ampoules, improved bukhary, aluminium bins and phosphide use. The respondents of Bulandshahr district have assigned second rank to grinding and mixing technology whereas respondents of Rampur district assigned second rank to ironing clothes. Kunwar et al. (1991-94) have observed in a study of Rampur district that 65.15 per cent landless rural women did not give much importance to washing clothes because of ever increasing prices of soaps and detergents which they could not afford whereas 85.16 and 86.84 per cent women of small and large holding households, respectively, gave much importance to washing and ironing of clothes. The reason of showing high interest in ironing of clothes, as told by some respondents, was that they wanted members of their family should be well up-to-date, and also they could afford.

Table 5.40 Respondents showing interest in household technologies

Technology	Rampur		Bulandshahr		Pooled	
	Av. score	Rank	Av. Score	Rank	Av. Score	Rank
Cooking	0.38	IV	0.14	V	0.28	IV
Washing clothes	0.06	VI	0.17	IV	0.11	VI
Ironing clothes	0.44	II	0.24	III	0.34	III
House cleaning	0.35	V	0.09	VI	0.22	V
Grain storage	0.78	I	0.80	I	0.79	I
Grinding/mixing	0.43	III	0.49	II	0.46	II
F-value for	Districts				1.41 ($p > 0.05$)	
	Technologies				8.96 ($P < 0.05$)	
Spearman's rank Correlation					0.77 ($P < 0.001$)	

Assigning second rank to grinding and mixing technology by respondents of Bulandshahr district was on account of their view that cooking and grinding of spices are essential for sumptuous delicious meal.

The pattern of interest shown by respondents of the two districts was found to be non-significant. Spearman's rank correlation confirms this result that rankings are closely related.

(c) Adoption of technologies

Adoption of modern farm, animal husbandry and household technologies was assessed and analysed.

(i) Farm technologies

Adoption level and adoption index were calculated for farm technologies. Adoption level was divided into three categories – full, partial and no adoption. Adoption of more than 66 per cent of total practiced was categorised as full, and less than or equal to 66 per cent as partial adoption. Adoption index was calculated as mentioned in the research methodology.

(a) Wheat crop technologies

Table 5.41 reveals that 16.39 per cent respondents of Rampur district have full adoption of improved varieties whereas 22.41 per cent respondents of Bulandshahr district have full adoption of this technology. Overall, only 19.33 per cent respondents have full adoption of improved wheat varieties.

The table also reveals that 49.18 per cent respondents of Rampur district have full adoption of Fertilizers and manures technology. These respondents have efficiently applied fertilizers and manures in wheat crop. In sowing technology, 47.54 and 52.46 per cent respondents of Rampur district have full and partial adoption, respectively. The respondents though have knowledge of Plant protection measures and also have interest in its application but could not adopt this technology on account of hazardous application. Singh and Sharma (1991) have observed that in Uttar Pradesh plant protection, chemical weed control and land preparation are such activities which require more skills performed by men only.

(b) Paddy crop technologies

Table 5.42 shows that less than 20 per cent respondents of Bulandshahr district have full adoption of improved paddy

Table 5.41 Adoption level of technologies of wheat cultivation

(Horizontal percentage)

Technology	Rampur (n_1=61)			Bulandshahr (n_2 =58)			Pooled (N =119)		
	Full	Partial	No	Full	Partial	No	Full	Partial	No
HYV	16.39	34.43	49.18	22.41	46.55	31.04	19.33	40.24	40.33
Seed rate	37.70	50.82	11.48	36.21	50.00	13.79	36.97	50.42	12.61
Sowing	47.54	52.46	-	32.76	60.34	6.90	40.34	56.30	3.36
Fertilizers And Manures	49.18	34.43	16.39	34.48	44.83	20.69	42.02	39.50	18.48
Irrigation	39.34	37.70	22.96	39.66	48.27	12.07	39.50	42.85	17.65

Table 5.42 Adoption level of technologies of paddy cultivation

(Horizontal percentage)

Technology	Rampur (n_1=65)			Bulandshahr (n_2 =62)			Pooled (N =127)		
	Full	Partial	No	Full	Partial	No	Full	Partial	No
HYV	20.00	36.92	43.08	17.74	46.78	35.48	18.89	41.73	39.38
Seed rate	27.69	40.00	32.31	20.97	50.00	29.03	24.41	44.88	30.71
Nursery	21.54	47.69	30.77	14.52	45.16	40.32	18.11	46.46	35.43
Bed raising									
Seed bed Preparation	13.85	40.00	46.15	17.74	51.62	30.64	15.75	45.67	38.58
Transplanting Method	32.31	52.31	15.38	30.64	48.39	20.97	31.50	50.39	18.11
Fertilizers Manures	23.08	47.69	29.23	17.74	58.06	24.20	20.47	52.76	26.77

varieties. In transplanting, 32.31 per cent respondents of Rampur and 30.64 per cent respondents of Bulandshahr district have full adoption of transplanting practices.

Pooled analysis shows that between 35-50 per cent respondents have partial adoption of farm technologies and 15-31 per cent respondents have full adoption of farm technologies.

(c) Sugarcane crop technologies

It is evident from Table 5.43 that between 19-25 per cent respondents have full adoption of sugarcane crop technologies and between 47-70 per cent respondents have partial adoption of these technologies.

Table 5.43 also shows that 74.42 and 64.10 per cent respondents of Rampur and Bulandshahr districts, respectively, have partially adopted the improved sugarcane varieties. The reason of high percentage of respondents having partial adoption was that only up to 42.68 per cent respondents have knowledge of improved varieties and the rest ones have no knowledge, but working with men-folk they have adopted this technology. Next to improved varieties, the high percentage of respondents of Rampur and Bulandshahr have partial adoption of seed rate and Fertilizers and manures technologies.

Table 5.44 shows the average adoption indices of wheat, paddy and sugarcane technologies and range of adoption of technologies. It is evident from the table that average adoption of practices of technologies of wheat crop was ranged between 7 to 15 in Rampur district and between 7 to 14 in Bulandshahr district. This shows that there is no significant difference in adoption of practices. The non-significant t-value confirms this.

Comparing the adoption of sugarcane cultivation practices between two districts, it was found that there is significant difference in adoption. The range of adoption of practices in Rampur district was more that of Bulandshahr district.

(d) Animal husbandry technologies

For assessment of adoption of animal husbandry technologies by respondents, average score was calculated on the basis of frequency of using technology. Scale values of 2,1

Table 5.43 Adoption level of technologies of sugarcane cultivation

(Horizontal percentage)

Technology	Rampur (n_1=65)			Bulandshahr (n_2 =62)			Pooled (N =127)		
	Full	Partial	No	Full	Partial	No	Full	Partial	No
HYV	16.27	74.42	9.31	23.08	64.10	12.82	19.51	69.51	10.98
Seed rate	27.91	60.46	11.63	17.95	58.97	23.08	23.17	59.76	17.07
Fertilizers and manures	20.93	48.84	30.23	28.20	46.15	25.65	24.39	47.56	28.05
Irrigation	25.58	44.19	30.23	23.08	53.84	23.08	24.39	48.78	26.83

TABLE 5.44 ADOPTION INDICES OF FRAM TECHNOLOGIES

Crop	Rampur		Bulandshahr			Pooled	
	Av.-adoption index	± S.D.	Av.-adoption index	± S.D.	t-value	Av.-adoption index	± S.D.
Wheat	0.511	10.73 ± 3.56	0.486	10.51 ± 3.41	1.32@	0.501	10.62 ± 3.39
Paddy	0.479	15.35 ± 4.15	0.438	15.18 ± 3.94	0.168@	0.459	15.26 ± 3.81
Sugarcane	0.575	12.65 ± 4.19	0.383	10.82 ± 3.55	2.13*	0.483	11.77 ± 3.63

* $P < 0.05$; @ $P > 0.05$

and zero were assigned to regular, sometimes and never used, respectively.

Table 5.45 shows that deeding technology was the highly adopted by the respondents of Rampur district whereas preparation of milk products technology was highly adopted by the respondents of Bulandshahr district.

Table 5.45 Adoption of animal husbandry technologies

Technology	Rampur		Bulandshahr		Pooled	
	Av. Score	Rank	Av. Score	Rank	Av. Score	Rank
Breeding	0.20	VI	0.23	VI	0.21	VI
Feeding	1.49	I	1.05	II	1.27	I
Fodder growing	0.30	V	0.41	V	0.36	V
Health care	0.88	IV	0.71	IV	0.79	IV
Use of drug	1.03	III	0.81	III	0.92	III
Preparation of milk Products	1.07	II	1.10	I	1.08	II

F-value for	
Districts	1.71 (P> 0.05)
Technologies	16.08 (P< 0.001)
Spearman's rank Correlation	0.94 (P< 0.001)

The reason of the highest adoption of feeding technology by respondents of Rampur district that green fodder was easily available to them and they also used concentrated mineral mixture so that balanced diet might be provided to the animals. Muniratnam and Srilatha (1991) have also observed that women are more concerned to give balanced diet to the animals. Nearly 70-80 per cent women provided balanced diet to their animals. Regarding health care of animals, respondents of both the districts have placed it to fourth rank. This shows that they thought that health care of animals was the outlook of their men. Although, Muniratnam and Srilatha (1991) have reported that 70-80 per cent women in their study area, Chittoor district, have technological adoption for the health care of their animals, but this study does not show the similar finding. Only 30-35 per cent respondents under study have adopted health care practice and the rest were of the view that it came under men's purview.

Table 5.45 also shows highly significant value of Spearman's rank correlation and F-value for technologies. It means that the ranking are closely related and there is significant variation in the adoption scores between technologies.

(e) Household technologies

Adoption scores for different household technologies were calculated on the basis of frequency of their use. Scale values of 2, 1 and zero were assigned to regular, sometimes and never used, respectively.

Table 5.46 Adoption of household technologies

Technology	Rampur		Bulandshahr		Pooled	
	Av. Score	Rank	Av. Score	Rank	Av. Score	Rank
Cooking	1.41	III	1.26	II	1.20	II
Washing clothes	0.58	IV	0.42	V	0.50	VI
Ironing clothes	0.52	V	0.38	VI	0.90	IV
House cleaning	0.47	VI	0.71	IV	0.59	V
Grain storage	1.31	I	1.52	I	1.41	I
Grinding/mixing	1.20	II	0.85	III	1.02	III
F-value for						
Districts	–					
Technologies	11.62 (P< 0.001)					
Spearman's rank Correlation	0.77 (P< 0.001)					

The perusal of Table 5.46 reveals that respondents of both the districts have assigned the highest score to modern grain storage technology. Of the 46.5 per cent respondents having adopted this technology, 39.78 per cent have adopted it regularly and the rest have adopted it occasionally. Kunwar (1996) in a study of rural area of Kanpur has observed that if

Table 5.47 Factors affecting use of household technologies by respondents of Rampur district

(Number)

Modern technology	Unawareness	Non-availability of raw material	Proof financial position	Lack of technical know-how	Not suitable for the family	Costly application	Limited size of appl-ication	Not suitable for village life	Total
Cooking device									
(a) Smokeless Chulha	62 (73.82)	-	6 (7.14)	10 (11.90)	6 (7.14)	-	-	-	84
(b) Bio-gas burner	59 (68.60)	5 (5.81)	3 (3.49)	9 (10.47)	4 (4.65)	3 (3.49)	3 (3.49)	-	86
(c) Solar cooker	55 (63.95)	-	9 (10.47)	15 (17.44)	7 (8.14)	-	-	-	86
(d) Electric heater	13 (27.66)	18 (38.30)	11 (23.40)	-	5 (10.63)	-	-	-	47
(e) Microwave oven	74 (76.29)	19 (19.59)	-	-	4 (4.12)	-	-	-	97
(f) LPG burner	12 (28.57)	8 (19.05)	-	10 (23.81)	-	12 (28.57)	-	-	42
Washing machine	54	19	-	1	-	18	1	-	93

Electric iron	21 (24.42)	35 (40.70)	30 (34.88)	-	-	-	-	-	86
Vaccum cleaner	90 (91.84)	-	3 (3.06)	0	0	0	1 (1.02)	4 (4.08)	98
Grain storage	30 (69.77)	-	-	13 (30.23)	-	-	-	-	43
Grinder/mixer	55 (69.62)	18 (22.78	-	1 (1.27)	-	5 (6.33)	-	-	79
Bal bearing chakki	97 (97.98)	-	-	-	2 (2.02)	-	-	-	99

(Figures given in parenteses are horizontal percentages)

	(58.06)	(20.43)		(1.08)		(19.35)	(1.08)		

proper training is imparted to women, the adoption of modern grain storage technology may increase. In her study, after training 60 per cent women adopted EDB ampoules whereas it was only 43.33 per cent prior the training was imparted.

Respondents have assigned second rank to cooking devices and third rank to grinders and mixers. They have assigned fourth, fifth and sixth ranks to ironing, house cleaning and washing of clothes, respectively. In their view, these practices are not very essential in village life where surroundings are, generally, dusty. They have not shown much interest in adoption of technology developed for these.

The analysis of factors affecting the use of modern household technologies reveals that high percentage of respondents of Rampur and Bulandshahr districts were unaware of modern household technologies (Table 5.47 and Table 5.48). Of the modern cooking appliances, 76.29 per cent respondents of Rampur and 89.70 per cent of Bulandshahr district have no knowledge about microwave oven. Those who have knowledge of microwave oven could not adopt it regularly on account of irregular electric supply to their villages. Drastic power cut have forced those households who have invested huge amount in purchase of electric-operated modern appliances for their comfort to keep them as a show piece.

Next to lack of awareness and non-availability of raw-material, poor financial position, lack of technical know-how and costly application are the other main factors affecting the adoption of modern technologies. Kaur and Sharma (1991) have also reported that women of Haryana state did not adopt modern household technologies on account of lack of awareness, economic difficulties and complexity in the use. During the study, it was also observed that smokeless chulha, a very simple device, has not been adopted by 84 and 92 per cent respondents of Rampur and Bulandshahr districts, respectively, on account of poor financial position, lack of technical know-how and unsuited for the family.

Devdas (1991) have stated that any technology, be it simple, complex or sophisticated, would prove its utility only to the extent it is indigenous, suitable, meeting the needs of the user, and in tune with the resources available and the culture.

Table 5.48 Factors affecting use of household technologies by respondents of Bulandshahr district

(Number)

Modern technology	Unawareness	Non-availability of raw material	Proof financial position	Lack of technical know-how	Not suitable for the family	Costly application	Limited size of appl-ication	Not suitable for village life	Total
Cooking device									
(a) Smokeless Chulha	57 (61.96)	-	12 (13.04)	18 (19.57)	5 (5.43)	-	-	-	92
(b) Bio-gas burner	41 (56.16)	-	13 (17.81)	3 (4.11)	-	- (21.92)	16	-	73
(c) Solar cooker	62 (76.54)	-	3 (3.70)	15 (18.52)	-	1 (1.24)	-	-	81
(d) Electric heater	32 (49.23)	14 (21.54)	15 (23.08)	3 (4.61)	-	1 (1.54)	-	-	65
(e) Microwave oven	87 (89.70)	5 (5.15)	-	-	5 (5.15)	-	-	-	97
(f) LPG burner	19 (48.72)	-	12 (30.77)	-	8 (20.51)	-	-	-	39

(contd.)

Modern technology	Unawareness	Non-availability of raw material	Proof financial position	Lack of technical know-how	Not suitable for the family	Costly application	Limited size of appl-ication	Not suitable for village life	Total
Washing machine	41 (44.56)	18 (19.56)	-	21 (22.83)	-	7 (7.61)	-	5 (5.44)	92
Electric iron	19 (21.59)	43 (48.86)	26 (29.54)	-	-	-	-	-	88
Vaccum cleaner	85 ((86.73)	-	-	-	-	4 (4.08)	-	9 (9.19)	98
Grain storage	39 (60.94)	-	-	25 (39.06)	-	-	-	-	64
Grinder/mixer	43 (52.44)	12 14.63)	8 (9.77)	3 3.66)	-	6 (7.32)	10 (12.18)	-	82
Bal bearing chakki	100 (100.00)	-	-	-	-	-	-	-	100

(Figures given in parenteses are horizontal percentages)

Table 5.49 Factors affecting use of household technologies by respondents of Rampur and Bulandshahr district

(Number)

Modern technology	Unawareness	Non-availability of raw material	Proof financial position	Lack of technical know-how	Not suitable for the family	Costly application	Limited size of appl-ication	Not suitable for village life	Total
Cooking device									
(a) Smokeless Chulha	119 (67.61)	-	18 (10.23)	28 (15.91)	11 (6.25)	-	-	-	176
(b) Bio-gas burner	100 (62.89)	5 (3.14)	16 (10.06)	12 (7.54)	4 (2.52)	3 (1.89)	19 (11.96)	-	159
(c) Solar cooker	117 ((70.06)	-	12 (7.19)	30 (17.96)	7 (4.19)	1 (0.60)	-	-	167
(d) Electric heater	45 (40.18)	32 (28.57)	26 (23.22)	3 (2.68)	5 (4.46)	1 (0.89)	-	-	112
(e) Microwave oven	161 ((82.99)	24 (12.37)	-	-	9 (4.64)	-	-	-	194
(f) LPG burner	31 ((38.27)	8 (9.88)	12 (14.81)	10 (12.35)	8 (9.88)	12 (14.81)	-	-	81

(contd.)

Modern technology	Unawareness	Non-availability of raw material	Proof financial position	Lack of technical know-how	Not suitable for the family	Costly application	Limited size of appl-ication	Not suitable for village life	Total
Washing machine	95 (51.35)	37 (20.00)	-	22 (11.89)	-	25 (13.52)	1 (0.54)	5 (2.70)	185
Electric iron	40 (22.99)	78 (44.83)	56 (32.18)	-	-	-	-	-	174
Vaccum cleaner	175 (89.29)	-	3 (1.53)	-	-	4 (2.04)	1 (0.51)	13 (6.63)	196
Grain storage	69 (64.48)	-	-	38 (35.52)	-	-	-	-	107
Grinder/mixer	98 (60.87)	30 (18.63)	8 (4.97)	4 (2.48)	-	11 (6.83)	10 (6.22)	-	161
Bal bearing chakki	197 (98.99)	-	-	-	2 (1.01)	-	-	-	199

(Figures given in parenteses are horizontal percentages)

III. ROLE AND STATUS OF WOMEN

In the past, status was referred to some of the capacities which could be legally enforced and also to some the limitations of persons and their relative superiority and inferiority. Now the term has undergone radical changes and it has become a synonym for any position in social system (Lal, 1987).

Role and status are two inter-related terms. While status defines who a person is, role defines what such a person is expected to do. Thus, status of a person very much depends upon the role or roles he or she has to perform.

Table 5.50 Role of women of Rampur district in farm operations

(Horizontal percentage)

Operation	Family income group (Rs.) Below 50,000 (n_1=55)			50,000-1,00,000 (n_2=32)			Above 1,00,000 (n_3=13)		
	D	S	N	D	S	N	D	S	N
Sowing/ Transplanting	21	17	17	13	10	9	5	4	4
Nursery bed Raising	7	9	39	4	5	23	2	2	9
Interculture	33	15	7	19	9	4	9	3	1
Fertilizers application	4	18	33	2	11	19	1	4	8
Irrigation	4	18	33	3	11	18	1	4	8
Harvesting	26	14	15	16	9	7	7	4	2
Threshing	8	36	11	4	21	7	2	8	3

D = Dominating role; S = Supporting role; N = No role

Like men, women occupy many status position in a given system and play a number of roles such as those in kinship system and, family system and wider social system. Their position in the society must not be determined by one particular status position they hold, but by their composite status in ritual hierarchy.

Table 5.51 Role of women of Bulandshahr district in farm operations

(Horizontal percentage)

Operation	Family income group (Rs.) Below 50,000 (n_1=48)			50,000-1,00,000 (n_2=35)			Above 1,00,000 (n_3=17)		
	D	S	N	D	S	N	D	S	N
Sowing/ Transplanting	21	16	11	17	15	3	3	7	7
Nursery bed Raising	6	13	29	10	7	18	1	1	15
Interculture	31	15	2	20	12	3	2	4	11
Fertilizers Application	5	13	30	12	21	2	2	4	11
Irrigation	6	11	31	4	8	23	1	2	14
Harvesting	29	14	5	17	12	6	9	5	3
Threshing	10	21	17	5	19	11	6	8	3

D = Dominating role; S = Supporting role; N = No role

Women have an equal contribution to make in every sphere of human development activity, be it agriculture, industry, services or business, their role can not be minimized. They play a significant and crucial role not only in agricultural development and allied fields including crop production, livestock production, horticulture, etc. but also in non-farm operations and household activities.

(a) Farm operations

In traditional village community, the women have been playing a distinctive accepted role in the crop production. Agriculture is still a family endeavour, but pattern of women's participation vary according to regional and cultural norms.

In western Uttar Pradesh, rural woman does every kind of field work except ploughing. She supports the man in some field works and in some works she dominates also by doing

Table 5.52 Homogeneity of correlation coefficients

Operation	Correlation coefficient		Z-value	Coefficient of alienation (k)	
	Rampur	Bulandshahr		Rampur	Bulandshahr
Sewing/ Transplanting	0.0134	-0.1376	0.871	0.999	0.990
Nursing bed raising	0.0127	-0.083	0.668	0.999	0.996
Interculture	0.0519	-0.4791***	3.995**	0.998	0.878
Fertilizers application	0.3581***	0.1534	1.533	0.933	0.988
Irrigation	-0.2293*	-0.1117	0.844	0.973	0.994
Harvesting	0.0776	-0.0981	1.227	0.997	0.995
Threshing	-0.0225	0.1298	1.107	0.999	0.991

*P <0.05 **P <0.01 ***P < 0.001

more than 66 per cent of operations. Table 5.50 reveals that 61 per cent respondents of Rampur district have dominated intercultural operations, 49 per cent harvesting and 39 per cent transplanting operations. Sardana et al. (1988) have observed that 59.67 per cent women have dominating role in weeding operation, 49.66 per cent in harvesting and only 2.67 per cent in threshing operations. Family income-wise, 69.23 per cent respondents of high income group (above Rs. 1 lakh) families dominated the intercultural operations whereas approximately equal percentage of respondents of middle and lower income group families have dominated the intercultural operations. This shows that in Rampur district, women of high income group households participate actively in intercultural, harvesting and transplanting operations. Kunwar et al. (1991-94) have observed that 60.61 per cent rural women of Rampur district participated in harvesting operations belonged to landless class, 76 per cent to marginal and 88.89 per cent to small land holding households. Table 5.51 does not depict the similar trend. It shows that in Bulandshahr district only 11.76 per cent respondents of high income group households dominated the intercultural operations, 17.65 per cent transplanting and 52.94 per cent harvesting operations. Table 5.52 confirms these findings. Now-significant low degree correlation coefficients for these operations were observed in Rampur district whereas highly significant correlation coefficient was observed in intercultural operations in Bulandshahr district. Table 5.52 also shows high coefficients of alienation i.e. lack of relationship in all the farm operations. All but intercultural operations, correlation coefficients were found to be homogeneous. This indicates that role of women in farm operations in both the districts was almost similar.

Pooled data (Table 5.53) show that 62.13 per cent respondents of low income households have dominated role in intercultural operations, 55.39 per cent in harvesting and 40.78 per cent in transplanting. It was also observed that there were negative non-significant relationship between role of women and household income group in transplanting, irrigation, and nursery bed raising whereas significant in intercultural operations and non-significant positive relationship in harvesting operation (Table 5.54).

Table 5.53 Role of women of Rampur and Bulandshahr districts in farm operations

(Horizontal percentage)

Operation	Family income group (Rs.)								
	Below 50,000 (n_1=103)			50,000-1,00,000 (n_2=67)			Above 1,00,000 (n_3=30)		
	D	S	N	D	S	N	D	S	N
Sowing/ Transplanting	21.00	16.50	14.00	15.00	12.50	6.00	4.00	5.50	5.50
Nursery bed raising	6.50	11.00	34.00	7.00	6.00	20.50	1.50	1.50	12.00
Interculture	32.00	15.00	4.50	19.50	10.50	3.50	5.50	3.50	6.00
Fertilizers application	4.50	15.50	31.50	7.00	16.00	10.50	1.50	4.00	9.50
Irrigation	5.00	14.50	32.00	3.50	9.50	20.50	1.00	3.00	11.00
Harvesting	27.50	14.00	10.00	16.50	10.50	6.50	8.00	4.50	2.50
Threshing	9.00	28.50	14.00	4.50	20.00	9.00	4.00	8.00	3.00

D = Dominating role; S = Supporting role; N – No role

Table 5.54 Correlation coefficients of pooled data

Operation	Correlation coefficient (r)	Coefficient of alienation (k)
Sowing/transplanting	-0.0551	0.998
Nursery bed raising	-0.0332	0.999
Interculture	0.233*	0.972
Fertilizers application	0.0961	0.995
Irrigation	-0.0561	0.0998
Harvesting	0.0008	0.999
Threshing	0.0607	0.998

*P< 0.05

(b) Animal husbandry

Besides role in farm operations, women play active role in animal husbandry activities. Agarwal (1987) reported that the involvement and participation of rural women were more in animal husbandry than in agriculture. Kunzru and Tripathi (1999) stated that a nucleus of dairy unit more or less exists as a source of draught power. It is a traditional component in almost every household and it is secondary source of employment and income. The role of women in animal husbandry enterprise varies widely from region to region on account of varying agro-climatic conditions, cropping seasons and socio-economic and cultural variations.

Table 5.55 Role of women of Rampur district in animal husbandry operations

(Horizontal percentage)

Operation	Family income group (Rs.) Below 50,000 (n_1=55)			50,000-1,00,000 (n_2=32)			Above 1,00,000 (n_3=13)		
	D	S	N	D	S	N	D	S	N
Carrying fodder	39	14	2	17	10	5	-	5	8
Chaffing fodder	12	23	20	4	12	16	2	4	7
Feeding	27	22	6	9	12	11	1	5	7
Milking	30	14	11	7	19	6	2	8	3
Cattle care	18	24	13	12	14	6	2	7	4
Preparation of milk Products	20	24	11	15	11	6	9	4	-
Preparation of dung cakes	32	17	6	3	11	8	-	-	13
Marketing	27	14	14	7	16	9	-	2	11

D = Dominating role; S= Supporting role; N = No role

The analysis of role dynamics of respondents of Rampur district in relation to productivity of dairy animals revealed that respondents of high income group have, generally, supportive role in carrying fodder and feeding (vertical percentage 38.46), cattle care (vertical percentage 53.85) and milking (vertical percentage 61.54) (Table 5.55). Jamal (1989) has also observed that in feeding, cattle management and milk products preparation performance of women was at a high level. Table 5.55 also reveals that respondents of low income group households have dominating role in almost all activities under study whereas respondents of middle income group have dominated role in fodder carrying, preparation of milk products and cattle care. This shows that role performance in animal husbandry sector is affected by socio-economic status of the household.

Table 5.56 Role of women of Bulandshahr district in animal husbandry operations

(Horizontal percentage)

Operation	Family income group (Rs.) Below 50,000 (n_1=55)			50,000-1,00,000 (n_2=32)			Above 1,00,000 (n_3=13)		
	D	S	N	D	S	N	D	S	N
Carrying fodder	36	12	-	15	17	3	-	3	14
Chaffing fodder	9	20	19	3	11	21	-	2	15
Feeding	24	19	5	11	13	11	2	6	9
Milking	27	17	4	8	21	6	3	11	3
Cattle care	14	23	11	11	17	7	3	9	5
Preparation of milk products	17	21	10	19	11	5	7	4	6
Preparation of dung cakes	30	14	4	2	19	14	-	-	17
Marketing	26	13	9	6	19	10	-	3	14

D =Dominating role; S = Supporting role; N = No role

Table 5.56 reveals the similar results. It shows that respondents of high income group households of Bulandshahr district have supportive role in milking, cattle care and feeding while they have dominating role in milk products preparation. Respondents of low income group households have dominating role in carrying fodder (vertical percentage 75), milking (vertical percentage 56.25) and feeding (vertical percentage 50). Malik et al. (1999) reported that women devoted maximum time of the day in preparation of feed and in cattle feeding and take support of men in chaff cutting and milk sale.

Table 5.57 shows highly significant negative relationship between role of respondents and household income groups of Rampur district in carrying fodder, feeding preparation of cow dung cakes, and marketing operation. For Bulandshahr district, highly significant negative relationship was observed in carrying fodder, feeding, preparation of dung cakes and marketing operations. All but carrying fodder and marketing correlation coefficients are homogeneous. High level of lacking in relationship was observed in cattle care operations in both the districts.

Table 5.57 Homogeneity of correlation coefficients

Operation	Correlation coefficient (r)		Z-value	Coefficient of alienation (k)	
	Rampur	Buland-shahr		Rampur	Buland-shahr
Carrying fodder	-0.5321***	-0.7062***	1.992*	0.847	0.708
Chaffing fodder	-0.1432	-0.3141**	1.574	0.990	0.935
Feeding	-0.3942***	-0.3852***	0.070	0.919	0.923
Milking	-0.2283*	-0.2153*	0.097	0.974	0.977
Cattle care	-0.0621	0.0654	0.021	0.998	0.998
Preparation of milk products	0.2182*	0.0141	1.441	0.976	0.999
Preparation of dung cakes	-0.662***	-0.7221***	0.808	0.749	0.692
Marking	-0.410***	-0.8382***	5.418**	0.912	0.546

* P< 0.05** P< 0.01 ***P< 0.001

Pooled data (Table 5.58) analysis shows that 53.33 per cent (Vertical) respondents of high-income group households have dominating role in preparation of milk products. In other activities, respondents of high income group have, generally, supportive role. Respondents of low income group households have dominating roles, ranging between vertical per cent 20 to 73, in almost all the activities under study. Table 5.59 reveals all but milk products preparation operation correlation coefficients highly significant an negative. This indicates that with increase in household income the role of women in animal husbandry operations decreases.

Table 5.58 Role of women of Rampur and Bulandshahr districts in animal husbandry operations

(Horizontal percentage)

Operation	Family income group (Rs.)								
	Below 50,000 (n_1=103)			50,000-1,00,000 (n_2=67)			Above 1,00,000 (n_3=30)		
	D	S	N	D	S	N	D	S	N
Carrying fodder	37.50	13.00	1.00	16.00	13.50	4.00	-	4.00	11.00
Chaffing fodder	10.50	21.50	19.50	3.50	11.50	18.50	1.00	3.00	11.00
Feeding	25.50	20.50	5.50	10.00	12.50	11.00	1.50	5.50	8.00
Milking	28.50	15.50	7.50	7.50	20.00	6.00	2.50	9.50	3.00
Cattle care	16.00	23.50	12.00	11.50	15.50	6.50	2.50	8.00	4.50
Preparation of milk products	18.50	22.50	10.50	17.00	11.00	5.50	8.00	4.00	3.00
Preparation of dung cakes	31.00	15.50	5.00	2.50	15.00	16.00	-	-	15.00
Marketing	26.50	13.50	11.50	6.50	17.50	9.50	-	2.50	12.50

D = Dominating role; S = Supporting role; N =No role

Table 5.59 Correlation coefficients of pooled data

Operation	Correlation coefficient (r)	Coefficient of alienation (k)
Carrying fodder	-0.623***	0.782
Chaffing fodder	-0.254**	0.967
Feeding	-0.391***	0.920
Milking	-0.261**	0.965
Cattle care	-0.065	0.998
Preparation of milk product	-0.108	0.994
Preparation of dung cakes	-0.690***	0.724
Marketing	-0.466***	0.885

**P< 0.01; ***P< 0.001

(b) Household activities

Recognition of crucial roles of rural women in agricultural and allied fields should not obscure the fact that they continue to be concerned with their functions as homemakers. They, in general, put up approximately 5000 hours in a year for work i.e. at the rate of 14 hours/day minus some hours for contingencies (Varma and Malik, 1984). On an average, they spent 7 to 8 hours per day in household activities. They perform multiple duties by combining all types of household work with such other jobs depending upon the opportunities affected by the complex socio-economic and organizational structure of the life.

Table 5.60 reveals that all the respondents of high income group households did not have any role in fetching fuel whereas only 23.08 per cent (vertical) respondents of this group have supportive role in fetching water. The reason of not involving in fuel fetching was they took help of other persons. These respondents have high-dominated roles in child-care and health care of family members and own self. About 84.61 per cent (vertical) respondents of this group have dominating role in family budget making with husbands.

Respondents of low income group households have high dominating roles in fetching water, household cleaning and fetching fuel activities while high supportive roles in food preparation, stitching and sewing and health care of family members and own self. Food preparation, child care, health care of family members and fetching water are daily routine activities performed by these respondents whereas household cleaning and fetching fuel are weekly activities.

Table 5.60 Role of women of Rampur district in household activities

(Horizontal percentage)

Operation	Family income group (Rs.) Below 50,000 (n_1=55)			50,000-1,00,000 (n_2=32)			Above 1,00,000 (n_3=13)		
	D	S	N	D	S	N	D	S	N
Fetching water	41	14	-	20	12	-	-	3	10
Fetching fuel	38	7	10	4	9	19	-	-	13
Food preparation	14	33	8	8	15	9	2	11	-
Household cleaning	41	10	4	13	19	-	4	9	-
Child care	18	20	17	3	19	10	9	4	-
Health care	17	22	16	15	14	3	8	5	-
Stitching & Sewing	10	31	14	21	6	5	-	13	-
Budgeting	7	20	28	12	3	17	11	2	-

D = Dominating role; S = Supporting role; N = No role

Respondents of high income group households of Bulandshahr district (Table 5.61) have no role in fetching water and fuel whereas they have high dominated role in health care of family members especially aged persons. In food preparation activity respondents of middle income group households have high dominated role.

Table 5.61 Role of women of Bulandshahr district in household activities

(Horizontal percentage)

Operation	Family income group (Rs.) Below 50,000 (n_1=48)			50,000-1,00,000 (n_2=35)			Above 1,00,000 (n_3=17)		
	D	S	N	D	S	N	D	S	N
Fetching water	38	10	-	22	13	-	-	-	17
Fetching fuel	26	21	1	4	10	21	-	-	17
Food preparation	10	32	6	17	14	4	4	13	-
Household cleaning	38	8	2	6	17	12	5	10	2
Child care	13	11	24	9	16	10	2	11	4
Health care	20	26	12	5	20	10	9	8	-
Stitching & sewing	8	30	10	23	7	5	4	10	3
Budgeting	5	15	28	16	5	4	3	9	5

D =Dominating role; S =Supporting role; N =No role

The analysis of pooled data (Table 5.62) reveals that 76.70 per cent (vertical) respondents of lower income group households have dominated roles in fetching water and house cleaning activities because they have no other members in the family to do these activities. The respondents of high-income group households have high supportive roles in food preparation, house cleaning and child care activities. Since these activities are arduous, monotonous, and isolating, thus, in order to save labour, respondents of high-income group households employ paid domestic aids. In medium and small-scale self-cultivating peasant households this facility can not be utilized on account of the lack of resources. Hence, they have to perform domestic and farm activities both.

Table 5.62 Role of women of Rampur and Bulandshahr districts in household activities

(Horizontal percentage)

Operation	Family income group (Rs.) Below 50,000 (n_1=103)			50,000-1,00,000 (n_2=67)			Above 1,00,000 (n_3=30)		
	D	S	N	D	S	N	D	S	N
Fetching water	39.50	12.00	-	21.00	12.50	-	-	1.50	13.50
Fetching fuel	32.00	14.00	5.50	4.00	9.50	20.00	-	-	15.00
Food preparation	12.00	32.50	7.00	12.50	14.50	6.50	3.00	12.00	-
Household cleaning	39.50	9.00	3.00	9.50	18.00	6.00	4.50	9.50	1.00
Child care	15.50	15.50	20.50	6.00	17.50	6.50	8.50	6.50	-
Stitching & sewing	9.00	30.50	12.00	22.00	6.50	5.00	2.00	11.50	1.50
Budgeting	6.00	17.50	28.00	14.00	9.00	10.50	7.00	5.50	2.50

D = Dominating role;S = Supporting role;N = No role.

Table 5.63 reveals highly significant negative correlation coefficients for fetching water and fetching fuel activities and positive correlation coefficients for child care activities. Except fetching fuel activity, correlation coefficients of other activities were homogeneous. This shows that respondents of both the districts have similar relationship between role and household income. As the household income increases, respondents of high income group households devote more time in domestic chores than farm and allied operations.

IV. DECISION-MAKING PATTERN

In Indian society, status of woman is a much debated question and there is no crystallized available to measure it objectively. For women, participation in decision-making process related to farm and household activities is a good indicator of their status.

TABLE 5.63 CORRELATION COEFFICIENTS FOR HOUSEHOLD ACTIVITIES

(Number)

Activity	Correlation coefficient (r)		Z-value	Correlation coefficient (r) for pooled data	Coefficient of alienation (k)		
	Rampur	Bulandshahr			Rampur	Bulandshahr	Pooled data
Fetching water	-0.6214***	-0.7320***	1.434	-0.6821***	0.783	0.681	0.731
Fetching fuel	-0.6304**	-0.7288**	3.252**	-0.6772***	0.776	0.684	0.736
Food preparation	-0.0235	0.1446	0.856	0.0681	0.999	0.989	0.998
Household cleaning	-0.2538*	-0.4322***	1.407	-0.3520***	0.967	0.902	0.936
Child care	0.2963**	0.3559***	0.460	0.1161	0.955	0.935	0.993
Health care	0.3017**	0.858	1.574	0.1864	0.953	0.996	0.982
Stiching & sewing	0.1828	0.2960**	0.188	0.1712	0.983	0.955	0.985
Budgeting	0.4246***	0.1562	1.031	0.3614***	0.905	0.988	0.932

* P < 0.05; ** P < 0.01; *** P < 0.001

The decision-making pattern in the family was analysed for household, farm and animal husbandry activities. Information on six farm activities, eight animal husbandry activities and nine home management activities were collected through interview schedule.

(a) Farm activities

Analysis of the decision-making pattern (Table 5.64) revealed that farm activities were more or less a male domain. In some activities such as sowing, post-sowing, harvesting and post-harvesting, husbands consulted their wives but in pre-sowing activity husbands were the key decision-makers in both the districts.

Wives (41.88%) were the key decision-makers in carrying farm produce activity. In Rampur district, 59.37 per cent husbands took decisions regarding harvesting activities in consultation with their wives whereas 53.69 per cent husbands in Bulandshahr district took decision jointly. The pattern of decision-making in both the districts was similar in all the activities (Table 5.65).

It was also observed during interview that in all the 15 high educational status households decisions were taken jointly in money related maters whereas in 53.12 per cent low educational status households decisions were taken jointly. In rest of the households of this category, husbands were the key decision-makers in all the money related activities. Punia et al. (1991) have also reported that in sale and purchase of land and cattle decisions in the family were taken jointly. Rajvanshi (1990) has observed that in money related matters educated working women have greater say than their uneducated counterparts.

(b) Animal husbandry activities

Eight major decision-making activities related with animal husbandry and dairying in the family were studied. The results are presented in Table 5.66. It was observed that carrying fodder, feeding, milking of animals, cattle care, preparation of milk products and dung cakes were the activities dome by women and decisions taken by them. Husbands were not consulted for

Table 5.64 Decision-making pattern for farm activities

(Vertical percentage)

Activity	Decision-maker Rampur (n1=96)			Bulandshahr (n2=95)			Pooled (N=191)		
	W	H	J	W	H	J	W	H	J
Pre-sowing	21.87	40.62	37.51	18.95	47.37	33.68	20.42	43.98	35.60
Sowing	19.79	31.25	48.96	23.16	37.89	38.95	21.47	34.55	43.98
Post-sowing	18.75	29.17	52.08	22.10	34.74	43.16	20.42	31.94	47.64
Harvesting	17.71	22.92	59.37	13.68	32.63	53.69	15.71	27.75	56.54
Post-harvesting	25.00	23.96	51.04	18.95	32.63	48.42	21.99	28.27	49.74
Carrying farm produce	43.75	39.58	16.67	40.00	34.74	25.26	41.88	37.17	20.95

W-Wife; H-Husband; J-Joint

performance and other related matters of these activities by wives. Unlike Puri (1972) and Thakur (1997) observations that, generally, in animal related activities husbands predominated the decision-making process in the families and wives were denied of their due share, this study shows that being shouldering about 80 per cent of dairy workload majority of decisions were taken by women.

Table 5.65 Z-values for farm activities

Activity	Decision-makers		
	Wife	Husband	Joint
Pre-sowing	0.501	0.943	0.552
Sowing	0.567	0.965	1.394
Post-sowing	0.575	0.816	1.239
Harvesting	0.768	1.508	0.795
Post-harvesting	1.013	1.337	0.362
Carrying farm produce	0.526	0.693	1.466

(All the Z-values are non-significant at 5 per cent level)

Comparing the decision-making pattern of both the districts, it was revealed (Table 5.67) that pattern of decision-making in cattle care was significantly different for wives and husbands whereas for chaffing fodder activities decisions taken jointly was significantly different. For other activities, the decision-making pattern was homogeneous.

(c) Household activities

The decision-making pattern in household activities is presented in Table 5.68. The decision-making pattern on domestic affairs is dominated by the women, irrespective of the castes, religion, income and education, table 5.68 reveals that decisions made for fetching water, household cleaning and stitching and sewing activities were dominated by wives in both the districts. Regarding child care, decisions were mad jointly by 52.89 per cent of total couples. Rajvanshi (1990) and Varma (1990) have reported that though child rearing is the domain of wives but husbands dominate in this activity. Husbands like

Table 5.66 Decision-making pattern for animal husbandry activities

(Vertical percentage)

Activity	Decision-maker Rampur (n1=96)			Bulandshahr (n2=95)			Pooled (N=191)		
	W	H	J	W	H	J	W	H	J
Carrying fodder	40.62	28.13	31.25	45.26	32.63	22.11	42.93	30.37	26.70
Chaffing fodder	21.87	40.63	37.50	33.68	45.26	21.06	27.75	42.93	29.32
Feeding	42.71	30.21	27.08	36.84	33.68	29.48	39.79	31.94	28.27
Cattle care	47.92	25.00	27.08	33.68	43.15	23.17	40.84	34.03	25.13
Milking	50.00	21.87	28.13	43.16	20.00	36.84	46.60	20.94	32.46
Preparation of milk products	77.08	12.50	10.42	72.63	10.53	16.84	74.87	11.52	13.61
Preparation of dung cakes	67.71	13.54	18.75	64.21	11.58	24.21	65.97	12.56	21.47
Marketing	47.92	19.79	32.29	41.05	23.16	35.79	44.50	21.47	34.03

W –Wife; H –Husband; J-Joint

that their *diktat* in child rearing should be accepted by wives. Husbands were of the view that in respect of children's health, their growth and education, wives should not make decisions on their own but should consult them.

Table 5.67 Z-values for animal husbandry activities

Activity	Decision-makers		
	Wife	Husband	Joint
Carrying fodder	0.647	0.678	1.439
Chaffing fodder	1.837	0.648	2.542*
Feeding	0.830	0.515	0.367
Cattle care	2.023*	2.700*	0.625
Milking	0.950	0.317	1.292
Preparation of milk products	0.710	0.428	1.300
Preparation of dung cakes	0.511	0.409	0.921
Marketing	0.958	0.567	0.511

*P< 0.05

Table 5.69 reveals that all the Z-values are found to be non-significant. It indicates the decisions mad e in all the household activities were homogeneous i.e. decision-making pattern is similar in both the districts.

V. INVOLVEMENT OF WOMEN IN FARM AND HOMESTEAD ACTIVITIES

In developing agrarian societies such as our own, women are traditionally a housewife who perform dual role. Most of the work performed by women, however, are directly or indirectly linked with the economic activities. Their work is a productive activity, even if unpaid, whereas agricultural work is considered totally productive, animal husbandry work as partially productive, house work is considered as totally unproductive work.

Table 5.68 Decision-making pattern for household activities

(Vertical percentage)

Activity	Decision-maker Rampur (n1=96)			Bulandshahr (n2=95)			Pooled (N=191)		
	W	H	J	W	H	J	W	H	J
Fetching water	40.62	29.17	30.21	43.16	27.37	29.47	41.88	28.27	29.85
Fetching fuel	22.92	23.96	53.12	18.95	29.47	51.58	20.94	26.70	52.36
Food preparation	32.29	26.04	41.67	37.89	30.53	31.58	35.08	28.27	36.65
Household cleaning	65.62	18.75	15.63	71.58	13.68	14.74	68.59	16.23	15.18
Child care	28.12	18.75	53.13	26.31	21.06	52.63	27.22	19.89	52.89
Health care	23.96	12.50	63.54	22.10	18.65	61.05	23.04	14.66	62.30
Stitching & sewing	73.96	7.29	18.75	72.63	9.48	17.89	73.30	8.38	18.32
Budgeting	19.79	44.79	35.42	15.79	43.16	41.05	17.80	43.98	38.22
Grain processing and storage	30.21	18.75	51.04	24.21	11.58	64.21	27.23	15.18	57.59

W –Wife; H –Husband; J -Joint

Table 5.69 Z-values for household activities

Activity	Decision-makers		
	Wife	Husband	Joint
Fetching water	0.356	0.276	0.112
Fetching fuel	0.675	0.862	0.213
Food preparation	0.812	0.690	1.456
Household cleaning	0.889	0.953	0.169
Child care	0.281	0.398	0.068
Health care	0.305	0.849	0.355
Stitching & sewing	0.208	0.544	0.154
Budgeting	0.724	0.227	0.802
Grain processing and storage	0.938	1.389	1.857

(All the Z-values are non-significant at 5 per cent level)

Women constitute a formidable part of work force in agriculture. They do not only attend to various field operations like sowing/transplanting, watering, weeding of crops and scaring birds but also are in complete charge of many harvest and post-harvest operations like harvesting, threshing, winnowing and storage. The tending of farm animals and saving farm yard refuse for use, either as fuel or manure, have all been predominatingly women's occupations.

Keeping in view the above aspects, the involvement of rural women in various activities can be classified and discussed as follows:

(a) Contribution in crop production

(b) Contribution in homestead activities.

(a) Involvement in crop production

Prior to analysing the women's productive activities in agriculture, it would be proper to have an overall view of women labour utilization in crop production. In this regard, Table 5.70 shows the relationship between the involvement of respondents in crop production and socio-economic variables. The results of the Table 5.70 show that all the correlation coefficients are negative and only two i.e. for family income and respondent's educational status are highly significant. This shows that respondents of low income group family and low educational status involved more in performing the farm roles expected of them effectively compared to others. Laxmi Devi (1991) and Singh (1968) have also reported the similar findings in their studies.

Table 5.70 Relationship between involvement in crop production and socio-economic variables

Socio-economic variables	Zero-order correlation coefficient (r)
Age	-0.0416
Education of respondents	-0.4347***
Castes	-0.0396
Land holding	-0.0936
Materials possessions	-0.1157
Family income	-0.5313***
Family educational status	-0.1615
Family-size	-0.0617

*** $P < 0.001$.

Employment pattern of respondents belonging to different income groups and educational status of households were analysed and the results are given in Table 5.71 and Table 5.72. It is evident from Table 5.71 that respondents on an average got an employment of 115.40 days per annum per head in crop production on the sampled households. Of this total, she got light employment in harvesting of the crops, followed by interculture and sowing/transplanting of crops. The employment level was marked to be slightly higher in Bulandshahr district as compared to Rampur district.

An examination of employment according to income-group of households shows that level of employment gave a declining trend with the increase in income of households. It was the highest being 123.40 days/annum/head in the lowest income group, 114.17 days in middle income group and the lowest 90.87 days in the large income group (Table 5.71). A similar trend was observed for the districts under study, with a little higher employment in Bulandshahr district.

Table 5.72 reveals that the level of employment of respondents showed a declining trend with the enhancement of respondent's educational status. The level of employment of rural women in crop production process was the highest being 121.62 days per annum in uneducated respondents which declined to 115.60 days in primary, 108.42 days in secondary and further to 94.50 days in above secondary level. This trend was also observed in both the districts under study.

The findings of the study revealed that women belonging to higher economic status households and of higher educational status have lower involvement in crop production process as compared to women of lower economic status households and of lower educational status. Their activities are confined within and, at best, around the homestead.

(c) Involvement in homestead activities

A homestead is a land owned or occupied by a dwelling unit of the household along with the adjoining area, including gardens, courtyard, etc. It provides a vital role for the existence of rural people. Rural women are involved in a wide range of activities include domestic and allied agricultural activities.

(i) Animal husbandry activities

On animal based tasks, women labour was used substantially. Employment of women in preparatory and supportive activities of agricultural sector was also found common in the study area. Such activities were generally, performed by the members of the family themselves. Activities like cake making, preparation of *ghee*, milking animals, removing cow dung from the cattleshed and feeding of animals were mostly done by the respondents. The employment position of respondents in such activities has been worked out and presented in Tables 5.73 and 5.74.

Table 5.71 Involvement of women in crop production activities according to income-group of households.

(Days per annum per head)

Farm operations	Rampur				Bulandshahr				Pooled			
	Below Rs.50000 (n_1=55)	Rs.50000-1,00,000 (n_2=32)	Above Rs.100000 (n_3=13)	Average	Below Rs.50000 (n_1=48)	Rs.50000-1,00,000 (n_2=35)	Above Rs.100000 (n_3=17)	Average	Below Rs.50000 (n_1=103)	Rs.50000-1,00,000 (n_2=67)	Above Rs.100000 (n_3=30)	Average
Sowing/ transplanting	22.00	20.50	16.00	20.74	23.50	21.50	16.50	21.60	22.70	21.02	16.28	21.15
Fertilizers and manures application	5.50	5.00	3.50	5.08	5.00	5.00	3.00	4.65	5.27	5.00	3.22	4.87
Intercultural operations	24.50	22.00	17.75	22.82	25.75	23.50	18.50	23.72	25.08	22.78	18.17	23.27
Irrigation	7.50	6.75	5.00	6.93	7.50	6.50	4.00	6.55	7.50	6.62	4.45	6.75
Harvesting	50.00	46.50	42.75	47.94	51.25	49.50	40.50	48.80	50.58	48.06	41.47	48.37
Threshing	9.50	7.25	5.00	8.19	9.00	9.00	5.50	8.40	9.27	8.16	5.28	8.30
Misc.	3.00	2.00	2.00	2.55	3.00	3.00	2.00	2.82	3.00	2.53	2.00	2.69
Total	122.00	110.00	92.00	114.25	125.00	118.00	90.00	116.54	123.40	114.17	90.87	115.40

Table 5.72 Involvement of women in crop production activities according to their educational status

(Days per annum per head)

Farm operations	Rampur					Bulandshahr					Pooled				
	UE (n_1=38)	PR (n_2=37)	SE (n_3=19)	AS (n_4=6)	Avg.	UE (n_1=26)	PR (n_2=55)	SE (n_3=17)	AS (n_4=2)	Avg.	UE (n_1=64)	PR (n_2=92)	SE (n_3=36)	AS (n_4=8)	Avg.
Sowing/ transplanting	20.75	21.00	19.75	18.50	20.52	21.50	20.00	20.00	16.00	20.30	21.05	20.40	19.86	17.88	20.41
Fertilizers and manures application	4.00	4.50	5.00	3.25	4.36	4.50	4.00	4.00	3.00	4.12	3.21	4.20	4.53	3.56	4.24
Intercultural operations	25.25	23.00	21.00	20.00	23.30	26.50	24.00	23.00	19.00	24.38	25.75	23.60	21.95	19.75	23.85
Irrigation	6.50	5.50	5.50	4.25	5.80	7.00	6.00	5.00	4.00	6.05	6.70	5.80	5.26	4.19	5.93
Harvesting	52.00	50.00	45.50	40.50	49.33	52.00	50.00	47.00	40.00	49.80	52.00	50.00	46.22	40.37	49.57
Threshing	9.00	8.00	7.25	6.00	8.13	9.50	9.00	8.00	6.00	8.90	9.20	8.60	7.60	6.00	8.50
Misc.	2.50	3.00	3.00	3.00	2.80	3.00	3.00	3.00	2.00	2.98	2.70	3.00	3.00	2.75	2.90
Total	120.00	115.00	107.00	96.00	114.24	124.00	116.00	110.00	90.00	116.54	121.62	115.60	108.42	94.50	115.40

UE = Uneducated; PR = Upto Primary; SE = Upto Secondary; AS = Above Secondary

Table 5.73 Involvement of women in animal activities according to income-group of households.

(Days per annum per head)

Activity	Rampur				Bulandshahr				Pooled			
	Below Rs.50000 (n_1=55)	Rs.50000-1,00,000 (n_2=32)	Above Rs.100000 (n_3=13)	Average	Below Rs.50000 (n_1=48)	Rs.50000-1,00,000 (n_2=35)	Above Rs.100000 (n_3=17)	Average	Below Rs.50000 (n_1=103)	Rs.50000-1,00,000 (n_2=67)	Above Rs.100000 (n_3=30)	Average
Animal grazing	10.00	7.00	-	7.75	12.00	8.50	-	8.74	10.93	7.79	-	8.25
Carrying fodder from field/forests	17.50	15.00	15.00	16.37	18.00	15.00	13.50	16.19	17.73	15.00	14.15	16.28
Fee preparation and feeding of animals	12.00	12.00	10.00	11.74	12.50	12.00	9.50	11.83	12.23	12.00	9.72	11.78
Animal care	7.50	6.75	6.00	7.06	8.00	7.00	7.00	7.48	7.73	6.88	6.57	7.27
Milking and sale of milk/milk products	11.50	12.25	12.00	11.80	12.25	11.00	11.50	11.69	11.85	11.60	11.72	11.76
Carrying FYM to field	7.50	6.00	4.00	6.56	8.25	7.50	4.00	7.28	7.85	6.78	4.00	6.91

Cleaning, filling, storage and preparation of food grains for marketing	5.50	6.00	5.00	5.60	6.00	6.00	4.00	5.66	5.73	6.00	4.42	5.63
Misc.	3.50	3.00	3.00	3.27	3.00	3.00	2.50	2.93	3.28	3.00	2.72	3.10
Total	75.00	68.00	55.00	70.15	80.00	70.00	52.00	71.80	77.33	69.05	53.30	70.98

Table 5.74 Involvement of women in crop production activities according to their educational status

(Days per annum per head)

Activity	Rampur					Bulandshahr					Pooled				
	UE (n_1=38)	PR (n_2=37)	SE (n_3=19)	AS (n_4=6)	Avg.	UE (n_1=26)	PR (n_2=55)	SE (n_3=17)	AS (n_4=2)	Avg.	UE (n_1=64)	PR (n_2=92)	SE (n_3=36)	AS (n_4=8)	Avg.
Animal grazing	11.00	10.00	7.75	4.50	9.62	12.00	11.00	8.00	3.50	10.60	11.40	10.60	7.87	4.25	10.12
Carrying fodder from field/forests	16.00	15.00	14.00	13.50	15.10	16.50	16.00	13.00	10.00	15.50	16.20	15.60	13.53	12.62	15.30
Feed preparation and feeding of animals	12.00	11.50	11.50	11.00	11.66	12.00	11.00	11.00	11.00	11.27	12.00	11.20	11.26	11.00	11.46
Animal care	7.00	7.00	7.00	6.50	6.97	7.00	6.50	6.00	6.00	6.53	7.00	6.70	6.53	6.37	6.75
Milking and sale of milk/milk products	12.00	11.00	11.00	10.75	11.36	12.00	11.50	11.00	11.00	11.53	12.00	11.30	11.00	10.81	11.45
Carrying FYM to field	7.00	6.50	5.75	5.00	6.46	8.00	7.00	7.00	6.00	7.24	7.42	6.80	6.34	5.25	6.85

Cleaning, filling, storage and preparation of food grains for marketing	6.00	6.00	6.00	6.00	6.00	6.50	6.00	6.00	6.00	6.13	6.20	6.00	6.00	6.00	6.06
Misc.	3.00	3.00	3.00	2.75	2.98	3.00	3.00	3.00	2.50	3.00	3.00	3.00	3.00	2.70	2.99
Total	74.00	70.00	66.00	60.00	70.15	77.00	72.00	65.00	56.00	71.80	75.22	71.20	65.53	59.00	70.98

UE = Uneducated; PR = Upto Primary; SE = Upto Secondary; AS = Above Secondary

It is evident from Table 5.73 that in activities like animal grazing, bringing fodder from fields, feeding and care of animals, etc. women were solely employed. On an average, woman got an employment of 70.98 days/head/annum in allied agricultural activities. Amongst the different activities, the employment was the highest in carrying fodder, followed by feed preparation and feeding animals and milking etc. It was almost the same in both the districts under study.

Women employment in animal husbandry activities according to income-group of households shows that their employment in these activities declined with the increase in income of the households, which was the highest (77.33 days) in the lowest income group, and the lowest (53.30 days) in the highest income group (Table 5.73). A similar trend was observed in both the districts under study.

In case of respondents's educational status, women involvement gave a decreasing trend with the enhancement of educational status of respondents. The highest 75.22 days was observed in uneducated respondents and 59 days in above secondary passed respondents. This trend shows that with the increase in educational status and income of the households, women's involvement in field and allied agricultural activities decreases. Punia et al. (1991) have also stated that higher the socio-economic status, lesser was the participation and time devoted by women.

(ii) Household activities

Like other Indian rural women, respondents of both the districts keep themselves busy in the endless domestic chores, for most part of the day till night. They have to look after all the domestic affairs meant for women. Table 5.75 reveals that rural women spent substantial time in household activities. On an average, they spent 34.58 per cent of their time in preparation of food and 30.60 per cent in child care and personal work. Time spent in other household activities like fetching water, cleaning/washing, fuel collection and marketing, etc. ranged between 5.55 to 8.87 per cent of the total time (9.02 hrs). It is also evident from the table that with the increase in income of the household, respondents devoted more time tin domestic works. The same trend was found in both the districts.

Table 5.76 shows that with the enhancement of educational status of respondents, devotion in household works declined. Sethi (1990) have stated that women spend a total of 6.5 hours/ day in cooking and cleaning of the house and utensils and another hour in child care or the care of the aged.

On combining the various activities performed by respondents, it was observed that our of 24 hours of the day, a rural woman worked for 4.96 hours in crop production, 0.32 hours in non-agricultural activities and 9.02 hours in household works. The rest of the day, she spent in leisure time including rest (Table 5.77 an 5.78). In terms of percentage, time spent on agricultural, non-agricultural and household activities was 20.67, 1.33 and 37.58 per cent, respectively.

VI. Employment of women in agriculture and non-agriculture sectors

Modern technology in agriculture encompasses the use of improved seeds, balanced use of fertilizers, pesticides, machinery equipments and scientific managerial approach. It has brought structural changes in crop production. With the increase in productivity, the employment of both men and women has been affected. The employment position of rural women of different socio-economic groups of households under study has been examined and discussed here.

It is evident from Table 5.79 that women got a total employment of 198.58 days per annum per head in the study area. Of this, employment from agriculture sector was 186.38 days (93.85 per cent), while from non-agricultural sector it was 12.20 days (6.15 per cent) only. Break-up of agriculture sector shows that the employment in crop production was to the extent of 115.40 days (61.92 per cent) while from allied agricultural activities it was 70.98 days (38.08 per cent). Almost similar trend was observed in both the districts under study. However, total employment was higher (200.74 days) in Bulandshahr district as compared to Rampur district (196.40 days).

Table 5.75 Involvement of women in household activities according to income-group of households.

(Hrs. per day per head)

Activity	Rampur				Bulandshahr				Pooled			
	Below Rs.50000 (n_1=55)	Rs.50000-1,00,000 (n_2=32)	Above Rs.100000 (n_3=13)	Average	Below Rs.50000 (n_1=48)	Rs.50000-1,00,000 (n_2=35)	Above Rs.100000 (n_3=17)	Average	Below Rs.50000 (n_1=103)	Rs.50000-1,00,000 (n_2=67)	Above Rs.100000 (n_3=30)	Average
Food preparation	3.00	3.00	2.75	2.97	3.20	3.50	3.00	3.27	3.09	3.26	2.90	3.12
Family care	2.50	3.00	3.50	2.80	2.60	2.75	3.10	2.75	2.55	2.87	3.27	2.76
Fetching water	0.50	0.50	0.50	0.50	0.50	0.50	0.50	0.50	0.50	0.50	0.50	0.50
Cleaning and washing	0.50	0.50	0.50	0.50	0.50	0.60	0.60	0.55	0.50	0.55	0.55	0.52
Fuel collection	0.75	0.50	0.50	0.64	1.00	0.70	0.50	0.80	0.87	0.60	0.50	0.72
Marketing	0.50	0.50	1.00	0.56	0.50	0.60	1.00	0.62	0.50	0.55	1.00	0.60
Other works	1.00	1.00	0.60	0.95	0.75	0.50	0.50	0.62	0.88	0.75	0.55	0.80
Total	8.75	9.00	9.35	8.92	9.05	9.15	9.20	9.11	8.89	9.08	9.27	9.02

Table 5.76 Involvement of women in household activities according to their educational status

(Hrs. per day per head)

Activity	Rampur					Bulandshahr					Pooled				
	UE (n_1=38)	PR (n_2=37)	SE (n_3=19)	AS (n_4=6)	Avg.	UE (n_1=26)	PR (n_2=55)	SE (n_3=17)	AS (n_4=2)	Avg.	UE (n_1=64)	PR (n_2=92)	SE (n_3=36)	AS (n_4=8)	Avg.
Food preparation	3.00	3.00	3.00	2.70	2.97	3.25	3.25	3.40	3.10	3.27	3.10	3.15	3.19	2.80	3.12
Family care	2.70	2.75	3.00	3.10	2.80	2.60	2.75	3.00	3.00	2.75	2.66	2.75	3.00	3.07	2.76
Fetching water	0.50	0.50	0.50	0.50	0.50	0.50	0.50	0.50	0.50	0.50	0.50	0.50	0.50	0.50	0.50
Cleaning and washing	0.50	0.50	0.50	0.50	0.50	0.50	0.60	0.50	0.50	0.55	0.50	0.55	0.50	0.50	0.52
Fuel collection	0.75	0.65	0.50	0.50	0.64	1.00	0.80	0.50	0.50	0.80	0.87	0.74	0.50	0.50	0.72
Marketing	0.50	0.50	0.65	1.00	0.56	0.50	0.60	0.80	1.00	0.62	0.56	0.55	0.72	1.00	0.60
Other works	1.00	1.00	0.90	0.50	0.95	1.00	0.50	0.50	0.50	0.62	1.00	0.70	0.70	0.50	0.80
Total	8.95	8.90	9.05	8.80	8.92	9.35	9.00	9.20	9.00	9.11	9.13	8.94	9.11	8.87	9.02

UE = Uneducated: PR = Upto Primary; SE = Upto Secondary; AS = Above Secondary

Table 5.77 Time utilization pattern of women in farm and homestead activities according to income-group of households

(Hrs. per day per head)

Activity	Rampur				Bulandshahr				Pooled			
	Below Rs.50000 (n_1=55)	Rs.50000-1,00,000 (n_2=32)	Above Rs.100000 (n_3=13)	Average	Below Rs.50000 (n_1=48)	Rs.50000-1,00,000 (n_2=35)	Above Rs.100000 (n_3=17)	Average	Below Rs.50000 (n_1=103)	Rs.50000-1,00,000 (n_2=67)	Above Rs.100000 (n_3=30)	Average
Agricultural	5.25	4.75	3.90	4.92	5.47	5.01	3.78	5.02	5.35	4.88	3.83	4.96
Non-agricultural	0.43	0.25	-	0.30	0.45	0.22	-	0.33	0.44	0.29	-	0.32
Household	8.75	9.00	9.35	8.92	9.05	9.15	9.20	9.11	8.89	9.08	9.27	9.02
Leisure time including rest	9.57	10.00	10.75	9.86	9.03	9.52	11.02	9.54	9.32	9.75	10.90	9.70
Total	24.00	24.00	24.00	24.00	24.00	24.00	24.00	24.00	24.00	24.00	24.00	24.00

Table 5.78 Time utilization pattern of women in farm and homestead activities according to their educational status

(Hrs. per day per head)

Activity	Rampur					Bulandshahr					Pooled				
	UE (n_1=38)	PR (n_2=37)	SE (n_3=19)	AS (n_4=6)	Avg.	UE (n_1=26)	PR (n_2=55)	SE (n_3=17)	AS (n_4=2)	Avg.	UE (n_1=64)	PR (n_2=92)	SE (n_3=36)	AS (n_4=8)	Avg.
Agricultural	5.17	4.93	4.60	4.16	4.92	5.36	5.01	4.66	3.90	5.02	5.25	4.98	4.64	4.09	4.96
Non-agricultural	0.45	0.40	-	-	0.30	0.43	0.40	-	-	0.33	0.44	0.40	-	-	0.32
Household	8.95	8.90	9.05	8.80	8.92	9.35	9.00	9.20	9.10	9.11	9.13	8.94	9.11	8.87	9.02
Leisure time including rest	9.43	9.77	10.35	11.04	9.86	8.86	9.59	10.14	11.00	9.54	9.18	9.68	10.25	11.04	9.70
Total	24.00	24.00	24.00	24.00	24.00	24.00	24.00	24.00	24.00	24.00	24.00	24.00	24.00	24.00	24.00

UE = Uneducated; PR = Upto Primary; SE = Upto Secondary; AS = Above Secondary

Table 5.79 Total employment of Women in different sectors according to income-group of households

(Days per annum per head)

Activity	Rampur				Bulandshahr				Pooled			
	Below Rs.50000 (n_1=55)	Rs.50000-1,00,000 (n_2=32)	Above Rs.100000 (n_3=13)	Average	Below Rs.50000 (n_1=48)	Rs.50000-1,00,000 (n_2=35)	Above Rs.100000 (n_3=17)	Average	Below Rs.50000 (n_1=103)	Rs.50000-1,00,000 (n_2=67)	Above Rs.100000 (n_3=30)	Average
(A) Agricultural	197	178	147	184.40	205	188	142	188.34	200.73	183.22	144.17	186.38
1. Crop production	122	110	92	144.25	125	118	90	116.54	123.40	114.17	90.87	115.40
2. Allied agricultural activities	75	68	55	70.15	80	70	52	71.80	77.33	69.05	53.30	70.98
(B) Non-agriculture	16	10	-	12	17	12	-	12.40	16.47	11.05	-	12.20
1. Non-agriculture wages	14.50	9	-	10.85	15.75	10	-	11.08	15.08	9.52	-	10.96
2. Trade/business	-	-	-	-	-	-	-	-	-	-	-	-
3. Service	-	-	-	-	-	-	-	-	-	-	-	-
4. Miscellaneous	1.50	1.00	-	1.15	1.25	2	-	1.32	1.39	1.53	-	1.24
Total (A+B)	213	188	147	196.40	222	200	142	200.74	217.20	194.27	144.17	198.58

Table 5.80 Total employment of Women in different sectors according to their educational status

(Days per annum per head)

Activity	Rampur					Bulandshahr					Pooled				
	UE (n_1=38)	PR (n_2=37)	SE (n_3=19)	AS (n_4=6)	Avg.	UE (n_1=26)	PR (n_2=55)	SE (n_3=17)	AS (n_4=2)	Avg.	UE (n_1=64)	PR (n_2=92)	SE (n_3=36)	AS (n_4=8)	Avg.
(A) Agricultural	194	185	173	156	184.40	201	188	175	146	188.34	196.84	186.80	173.95	153.50	186.38
1. Crop production	120	115	107	96	114.24	124	116	110	90	116.54	121.62	115.60	108.42	94.50	115.40
2. Allied agricultural activities	74	70	66	60	70.16	77	72	65	56	71.80	75.22	71.20	65.53	59.00	70.98
(B) Non-agriculture	17	15	-	-	12.00	16	15	-	-	12.40	16.60	15.00	-	-	12.20
1. Non-agriculture wages	15	13	-	-	10.50	14.50	14.00	-	-	11.47	14.80	13.60	-	-	11.00
2. Trade/business	-	-	-	-	-	-	-	-	-	-	-	-	-	-	-
3. Service	-	-	-	-	-	-	-	-	-	-	-	-	-	-	-
4. Miscellaneous	2	2	-	-	1.50	1.50	1.00	-	-	0.93	1.80	1.40	-	-	1.20
Total (A+B)	211	200	173	156	196.40	217	203	175	146	200.74	213.44	201.80	173.93	153.50	198.58

UE = Uneducated; PR = Upto Primary; SE = Upto Secondary; AS = Above Secondary

The above findings indicate that rural women have lower avenues of employment in non-agricultural sector as compared to agricultural sector. Employment of rural women in non-agricultural sector was found rare in the study area. However, in off-season, some women worked for non-agricultural wage earnings. The extent of such employment in both the districts was almost equal i.e. 12 days in Rampur and 12.40 days in Bulandshahr districts. It was found higher in lower income group households (Table 5.79) and in case of uneducated respondents (Table 5.80). One of the important cause for smaller opportunities of employment in non-agricultural sector may be male dominancy, their inherent shyness, lack of opportunities and unsuitability of jobs for women in rural area.

Unemployment position of rural women in both the districts in presented in Table 5.81. It is evident from the table that out of 300 days available for work during a year, rural women remain unemployed for 101.42 days (33.81 per cent) and employed for 198.58 days (66.19 per cent). In Bulandshahr district, as compared to Rampur district, the rural women were unemployed only for 99.26 days (33.09 per cent) in a year.

Table 5.81 Unemployment position of women

Particular	Rampur	Bulandshahr	Pooled
Total days available for work	300.00	300.00	300.00
Total employment days	196.40	200.74	198.58
Total unemployment days	103.60	99.26	101.42
Percentage of employment to Total days available	65.47	66.91	66.19
Percentage of unemployment to total days available	34.53	33.09	33.81

Usha et al. (1983) have observed that economic necessity is the most important factors for female labour participation but majority of them did not have ample time to work outside. Education was found to be the most important factor affecting the income from labour.

VII. IDENTIFICATION OF APPROPRIATE FARM TECHNOLOGIES

The Indian society is marked by inequities of the magnitude unseen elsewhere in the world. The uneven an unimpressive economic growth is also reflective of these inequities. The supply of appropriate technology to different segments of society especially to those living in vast rural areas is critical for mitigating the inequities and enhancing the economic growth.

Technology is a purposeful practical activity that involves the application of knowledge by organisation of human beings and their interactions with hardware. Technology represents the solutions to development and today technology has come to be raised to the status of an ideology. The ideology is that all the problems of human beings can be solved by appropriate application of technology.

Though in a limited aspect, technology has been understood as applying scientific knowledge to industrial process, abut in broader sense, it is the application of science to practical aim of life (Gupta, 2001). It refers to transformation of scientific laws into procedures and techniques to attain tangible ends for practical purposes.

The technology in broad sense, can be categorised as-

(i) High technologies i.e. capital and intensive energy,

(ii) Appropriate technologies i.e. low cost technologies using mainly local or easily available materials and skills.

(iii) Intermediate technologies i.e. small scale technologies emerging out of a gradual process of technological innovations sustainable in the communities.

Appropriate technology implies such technology that is suited to the economic and social conditions of practitioners and is in consonance with the level of civilization of the population (Chattopadhyay, 1998). One has to see such technology against waste of resources, destruction of environment and disturbance of socio-cultural equilibrium.

According to Dutt (2001), the criteria of technology appropriateness can be determined by taking into consideration the following factors :-

1. It should be compatible with local cultural and economic conditions.
2. The tools and processes should be accessible to people.
3. It should use locally available resources.
4. It should be ecologically and environmentally sound.
5. It should minimise cultural disruption and improve gender relations.
6. It should be flexible, efficient and labour intensive.
7. It should encourage participation of local community.

A technology is appropriate for women if it reduces their drudgery, improves their environment, their skills and enhances their comforts (Joshi and Rawal, 2001). Rural women play dual role. They perform agricultural and allied activities besides household activities. In this way, they devote approximately 14 hrs/day in performing activities. Bound in their traditional die-hard styles, they don't consider many of their back-breaking chores as 'laborious' or 'unjust'. It is primarily because for centuries, the male gender has been ruling as the family head. Thus, the plight of the women is constantly stooping down after so many decades of the country's development. The appropriate technological intervention can play important role to solve the problems or rural women.

In our country, agriculture is getting rapidly modernized in two ways: mechanization and improved agricultural technologies. Improved farm technologies encompasses improved seeds, balanced use of fertilizers, pesticides, machinery equipments and scientific managerial approach. Mechanization is meant not only to reduce drudgery but also to improve the efficiency of work.

For identification of appropriate farm technology which would provide maximum advantage to the rural women, the following four criteria have been considered:

(a) Enhancing production efficiency

(b) Income increasing

(c) Drudgery reducing

(d) Increasing community participation

(a) Production efficient technologies

To determine the farm and animal husbandry technologies which can enhance production, the selected farm women of the study area were asked to opine about the technologies which in their view may enhance production. Average scores were calculated and technologies were ranked.

Out of eight technologies of wheat, seven technologies of paddy crop and six technologies of sugarcane crop, they adjudged irrigation the most appropriate technology for enhancing wheat production, use of transplanter for paddy production and pre-sowing treatment for sugarcane production. The second technology in order of descending magnitude was improved varieties for wheat, paddy and sugarcane crops (Table 5.82). District-wise, the respondents of Rampur district adjudged improved varieties of wheat and sugarcane the most production efficient technology whereas the respondents of Bulandshahr district adjudged the irrigation the most appropriate technology for enhancing wheat and sugarcane and improved varieties for paddy production. It is true that use of improved varieties along with proper irrigation has enhanced the production of wheat, paddy and sugarcane crop.

Table 5.83 reveals that except sugarcane crop there was significant agreement in the opinions of women of both the districts of the efficiency of technologies of wheat and paddy crops. Regarding the variations in their opinions, it was found that there were no significant variations in the opinions of own of both the districts in respect to technologies of wheat, paddy and sugarcane. Between the technologies, there were significant variations in wheat and paddy crops, respectively.

Regarding efficient animal husbandry technology, respondents of both the districts adjudged breeding the most efficient one. They placed technology related with preparation of milk products the next best efficient technology (Table 5.84). Respondents of Rampur district adjudged breeding the most efficient technology but their counterparts of Bulandshahr did not agree with their opinions and they adjudged technology related with feeding the most efficient technology. Although there was high agreement in opinions of respondents of both the districts but no significant variations between opinion was pound. Between the technologies, there was significant variations in the opinion of respondents of Rampur as well as of Bulandshahr district.

Table 5.82 Production efficient farm technologies

Technology	Rampur Av. Score	Rampur Rank	Bulandshahr Av. Score	Bulandshahr Rank	Pooled Av. Score	Pooled Rank
(A) Wheat						
1. HYV	3.64	I	3.58	II	3.61	II
2. Sowing time	2.66	VII	3.01	VI	2.83	VI
3. Method of sowing	2.20	VIII	2.16	VIII	2.18	VIII
4. Fertilizers	3.49	III	3.56	III	3.52	III
5. Irrigation	3.54	II	3.71	I	3.62	I
6. Plant protection measures	2.74	V	2.68	VII	2.71	VII
7. Seed rate	2.72	VI	3.18	IV	2.95	V
8. Storage	3.28	IV	3.16	V	3.22	IV
(B) Paddy						
1. HYV	3.37	III	3.61	I	3.49	II
2. Seedbed	2.95	VI	2.63	VI	2.79	V
3. Transplanter used	3.46	I	3.54	III	3.50	I
4. Fertilizers	3.36	IV	3.13	IV	3.24	III
5. Irrigation	3.41	II	3.58	II	3.49	II
6. Plant protection measures	2.77	VII	2.61	VII	2.69	VI
7. Storage	3.00	V	3.03	V	3.01	IV
(C) Sugarcane						
1. HYV	3.32	I	3.35	IV	3.33	II
2. Method of ploughing	2.79	V	2.69	VI	2.74	VI
3. Fertilizers	3.12	III	3.37	III	3.24	IV
4. Irrigation	2.95	IV	3.64	I	3.29	III
5. Plant protection measures	2.72	VI	3.08	V	2.90	V
6. Pre-sowing treatment	3.28	II	3.53	II	3.40	I

Table 5.83 'F' and Spearman's rank correlation values

Crop	Districts		Technologies		Spearman's correlation coefficient	
	F-value	P-value	F-value	P value	r_s	P-value
Wheat	1.64	P>0.05	23.00	P<0.001	0.857	P<0.001
Paddy	-	P>0.05	10.71	P<0.05	0.859	P<0.001
Sugarcane	4.84	P>0.05	3.82	P>0.05	0.428	P>0.05

Table 5.84 Efficient animal husbandry technologies

Technology	Rampur		Bulandshahr		Pooled	
	Av. Score	Rank	Av. Score	Rank	Av. Score	Rank
Breeding	3.63	I	3.39	III	3.51	I
Feeding	3.28	III	3.45	I	3.36	III
Fodder growing	2.84	VI	2.91	VII	2.87	VI
Health care	3.00	V	3.14	V	3.07	V
Use of dung	2.47	VII	2.98	VI	2.72	VII
Milk products						
Preparation	3.40	II	3.41	II	3.40	II
Marketing	3.30	IV	3.16	IV	3.09	IV
F-values for						
Districts	2.76 (P>0.05)					
Technologies	41.20 (P<0.001)					
Spearman's rank correlation	0.931 (P<0.001)					

(b) Income increasing

The respondents of both of the districts adjudged improved varieties of wheat, paddy and sugarcane crops the most income increasing technology. In their opinion, use of improved varieties of these crops increased the income of their families. They were of the opinion that the balance use of fertilizers, proper and appropriate time of irrigation and improved varieties are the means of production (Table 5.85), Dhawan and Zohal

(1967) had observed that farm income can be increased through application of improved level of production techniques. Sinha (1980) opined that intensive cultivation, balanced use of fertilizers and irrigation had improved the family income and improved the standard of living of the landlord class women. The living standard of poor peasantry women has not changed because technological development has replaced them into non-agricultural activities.

Respondents of Rampur district, adjudged balanced fertilizers application and irrigation to the sugarcane crop second and third best income increasing technologies whereas their counterparts of Bulandshahr district showed reversed rankings. In their opinion, irrigation is more income increasing technology than balanced use of fertilizers.

The highly significant rank corrclation values indicate high agreement in their opinions and non-significant variance ratio for districts reveals no variation in their opinion. Highly significant variations were observed among the technologies of wheat and paddy crops, respectively (Table 5.86).

Table 5.85 Income increasing farm technologies

Technology	Rampur		Bulandshahr		Pooled	
	Av. Score	Rank	Av. Score	Rank	Av. Score	Rank
(A) Wheat						
1. HYV	2.82	I	2.71	I	2.76	I
2. Sowing time	1.66	VIII	1.71	VIII	1.68	VIII
3. Method of sowing	2.25	V	2.34	IV	2.29	V
4. Fertilizers	2.66	II	2.58	III	2.62	II
5. Irrigation	2.46	III	2.69	II	2.57	III
6. Plant protection measures	2.21	VI	2.16	VI	2.18	VI
7. Seed rate	2.16	VII	1.98	VII	2.07	VII
8. Storage	2.28	IV	2.32	V	2.30	IV

Technology	Rampur		Bulandshahr		Pooled	
	Av. Score	Rank	Av. Score	Rank	Av. Score	Rank
(B) Paddy						
1. HYV	2.51	I	2.59	I	2.55	I
2. Seedbed	1.97	VI	1.80	VII	1.88	VII
3. Transplanter used	2.37	IV	2.31	IV	2.34	IV
4. Fertilizers	2.48	II	2.37	III	2.42	III
5. Irrigation	2.43	III	2.49	II	2.46	II
6. Plant protection measures	2.15	V	2.18	V	2.16	V
7. Storage	1.86	VII	1.93	VI	1.89	VI
(C) Sugarcane						
1. HYV	2.21	I	2.44	I	2.32	I
2. Method of ploughing	1.84	VI	1.97	VI	1.91	VI
3. Fertilizers	2.16	II	2.33	III	2.24	III
4. Irrigation	2.12	III	2.39	II	2.26	II
5. Plant protection measures	2.02	V	2.10	IV	2.06	IV
6. Pre-sowing treatment	2.09	IV	1.98	V	2.03	V

Respondents of both the districts were of the opinion that preparation of milk products through application of modern technologies can improve income. The quality of these milk products would be more better than prepared through traditional techniques. Respondents were also of the view that breeding can improve family income.

Highly significant rank correlation coefficient shows that there is quite agreement in the opinion of respondents of both the districts. The respondents of each district showed significant variation in their opinions about technologies (Table 5.87).

Table 5.86 'F' and Spearman's rank correlation values

Crop	Districts		Technologies		Spearman's correlation coefficient	
	F-value	P-value	F-value	P value	r_s	P-value
Wheat	-	-	28.30	P<0.001	0.952	P<0.001
Paddy	1.63	P>0.05	14.13	P<0.001	0.928	P<0.001
Sugarcane	5.42	P>0.05	5.74	P>0.005	0.886	P>0.001

Table 5.87 Income increasing animal husbandry technologies

Technology	Rampur		Bulandshahr		Pooled	
	Av. Score	Rank	Av. Score	Rank	Av. Score	Rank
Breeding	2.42	I	2.36	II	2.39	II
Feeding	1.70	VII	1.84	VII	1.77	VII
Fodder growing	2.16	IV	2.19	IV	2.17	IV
Health care	2.13	V	2.11	VI	2.12	VI
Use of dung	2.12	VI	2.17	V	2.14	V
Milk products						
Preparation	2.39	II	2.51	I	2.45	I
Marketing	2.30	III	2.35	III	2.32	III
F-values for						
Districts			2.76 (P>0.05)			
Technologies			41.20 (P<0.001)			
Spearman's rank			0.930 (P<0.001)			

(d) Drudgery reducing

Drudgery is the physical strains and hardships experienced by human beings. Women's involvement in agricultural tasks by-and-large is a source of drudgery (Varma, 1989). Patriarchal society has assigned drudgery ridden agricultural task to women. Men have monopolized new agricultural technologies while women have not been encouraged to take these technologies and, hence, they are still using traditional method for food crops.

Table 5.88 Drudgery assigned to farm operations.

Operation	Rampur		Bulandshahr		Pooled	
	Scale value	Rank	Scale value	Rank	Scale value	Rank
Sowing behind Plough	0	V	0	V	0	V
Weeding	0.666	IV	0.349	III	0.716	IV
Transplanting	1.298	I	0.679	I	1.352	I
Harvesting	0.810	II	0.394	II	0.773	II
Carrying farm Produce	0.745	III	0.317	IV	0:739	III
Circular triades	0		0		0	
Absolute average Discrepancy (AD)	0.093		0.075		0.082	
Chi-square	14.32 (P< 0.05)		12.19 (P> 0.05)		24.36 (P< 0.05)	
Spearman's rank Correlation coefficient					0.903 (P< 0.001)	

A large number of women got involved themselves in drudgery ridden farm tasks only for supporting family income. Begum (1991) has also stated that women of Bangladesh got involved themselves in drudgery ridden agricultural tasks only for their own satisfaction and for increasing family income.

In crop production, the total amount of drudgery in carrying out agronomic operations of wheat and paddy crops shouldered by women is higher than that of own. Table 5.88 reveals that respondents of Rampur and Bulandshahr districts have assigned the highest scale value to transplanting operation of paddy crops. Thirty women of each district who were involved in wheat and paddy crops when shown paired pictures of farm operations assigned second rank to harvesting of crops. In harvesting, 52 per cent respondents of both the districts have dominating role i.e. they performed more than 66 per cent of harvesting work. Varma (1989) had observed that in wheat cultivation, women perform more drudgery ridden tasks than men whereas in paddy cultivation men perform more drudgery ridden tasks.

Table 5.89 Drudgery assigned to animal husbandry operations

Operation	Rampur		Bulandshahr		Pooled	
	Scale value	Rank	Scale value	Rank	Scale value	Rank
Carrying fodder	0.645	I	0.242	III	0.179	I
Fodder chaffing	0.424	III	0	V	0.043	IV
Feed preparation	0.541	II	0.430	II	0.076	II
Milking	0.381	IV	0.497	I	0.067	III
Preparation of cow Dung cakes	0	V	0.206	IV	0	V
Circular triades	0		0		3	
Absolute average Discrepancy (AD)	0.047		0.07		0.051	
Chi-square	5.13 (P>0.05)		10.23 (P>0.05)		10.48 (P>0.05)	
Spearman's rank Correlation coefficient0.85					(P< 0.001)	

Thus, the tasks in which women are exclusively involved and which consume more time and account for greater total drudgery are harvesting and transplanting.

The two sets of scale values for farm operation obtained form the respondents of both the districts are almost in agreement. The highly significant Spearman's rank correlation confirms this.

The drudgery scale values of the animal husbandry operations as assigned by respondents of Rampur and Bulandshahr districts were ranged between 0 to 0.645 and 0 to 0.497, respectively (Table 5.89). The respondents of Rampur district assigned the highest scale value of 0.645 to fodder carrying operations whereas their counterparts of Bulandshahr district assigned the highest scale value to milking operations. The pooled data reveal that respondents assigned the highest drudgery to fodder carrying operations. The reason of assigning highest drudgery to the operation was that carrying load of harvested fodder on their head created strained movement of eyes and neck. Thakur (1997) has also observed similar findings.

Grover and Kapoor (1998) have opined that modern agricultural technologies have displaced women to more skilled and drudgery ridden tasks. Mechanization is meant for drudgery reduction and to improve the efficiency of work. The introduction of hullers, improved sickles, transplanters, maize shellers, etc. are some of the devices which have been found useful for drudgery reduction. Thus souse of small hand driven wheel-cart would reduce drudgery in carrying fodder from field.

(e) Increasing community participation

It was observed that 62 per cent of total respondents have no membership in any social organisation in spite of adopting farm and animal husbandry technologies. The reason, as told by respondents, was lack of time and low level of education. This indicates that modern technologies have no any effect in raising the community participation of these respondents. Until and unless educational standard of respondents is enhanced and time saving technologies are evolved, there world be no significant increase in community participation.

CHAPTER 6

Socio-Economic Problems, Suggestions and Policy Implications

In our society, different values of home and work place maximise the differences in the instrumental roles of work place and expressive roles of home. Masculine and feminine stereotypes do not emerge from psychological differences between the two sexes but from social conditioning. A woman's socialisation posed obstacles in her self assertion, as dominant opinion in India held that a woman does not have much of a role to play outside the home, and if she does, this is her secondary role subject to the demands and exigencies of her role within the home.

PROBLEMS OF THE WOMEN

The women of Rampur and Bulandshahr districts face several socio-economic problems. The problems that emerge out form the existing ones are-

(1) Excess work load which is becoming less and less productive.

(2) Non-recognition as a decision-maker.

(3) Psychologically depressing environment

(4) Dependency on male members of the family

(5) Illiteracy resulting in lack of skills in conducting farming, family and social jobs.

(6) Being traditionalist, women did not think to accept new occupational avenues.

In the study area, in majority of households, women were playing only a secondary role in agriculture. They supported their men-folk in farm operations. To married working women with children, the martial relationship has become potentially a great stressor to them. Lack of time for husband, lack of emotional support, and competition between spouses were common problems faced by these women. Another major problem, in case of married women who worked outside the home, was work overload, resulting from conflicting demands associated with the multiple roles of wife, mother and career person. To some of them, over involvement in both the work and family roles was affected their health. They felt psychologically depressed. In low income group households, it was observed that some women were ill-fed and under continuous mental tension. After one full days labour outside home, when they come home in the evenings they were so tired that they could not do household work. non-fulfilment of household work tensionized them.

Economic dependence is the other problem faced by most of the women of the study area. The incidence of unemployment and illiteracy was high among these women. The assumption that their labour is unproductive or less productive, they were paid less wages than males for same work. These women, though less paid, also contributed full earnings in supplement of family income. Thus, they, for personal expenses, depended on men of the family like father, husband and sons.

The problem of non-recognition of women as a decision-maker was faced by less educated women. Many of their decisions were criticised and not taken into account by men-folk of their family. Even some men scoffed at their decisions. Being either only semi-educated or uneducated and submissive by nature, they lack the vocal power of convincing other s to accept and carry out their decisions.

Farming is a very complex pursuit requiring unskilled to highly skilled job. The illiteracy or low level of educational status forced women away from the highly skilled jobs.

Education plays a pivotal role in enabling a society to adopt and accept technology quickly is the proven fact. The maximum benefit of new modern technology could not be achieved by those women who have a little or no education, whatever benefit they have got from application of new modern technology was on account of their experience.

SUGGESTIONS

Women of the study area have to fight their own war by coming on the front line to accept the challenges faced by them. Even though, here are some suggestions to mitigate their sufferings.

1. For removal of work overload, work simplification methods should be evolved by the agricultural scientists and be introduced with simple mechanical aids whenever possible. If such aids are costly, they can be socially owned and used in turns with mutual agreed arrangements.
2. Women should know the essential technologies in the thrust areas like seed production, raising of nurseries, post-harvest technologies, storage of farm produce, crop and animal waste recycling, dairy and poultry management, etc. Several technologies have been developed but there is urgent need to disseminate them for strengthening and exploiting the hidden potential of women.
3. The infrastructure for dissemination of improved technologies and their use and benefits should be given in a package of know-how, raw material and supporting aids.
4. The technology should be indigenous and easily available to women.
5. The technology introduced for women should be aimed at reducing the drudgery involved in farm operations and household activities.
6. Appropriate technology should be introduced which may solve the fuel problems. Use of biogas technology, solar

cookers and thermal efficient cooking stoves should be made available to women.

7. Women should be made aware of the new agricultural tools and implements which can increase their productivity and at the dame time reduce drudgery. These implements like improved sickles, wheel hoes, maize shellers, transplanters, etc. have been tried out by agricultural engineers and were found suitable for women.

8. Demonstration and training camps for dissemination of the new technologies should be held fortnightly for women only in all the villages.

9. All efforts should be made to increase the active participation of women in technology generation, wherever required.

10. The nutritional status of working women should be given much importance in the family.

POLICY IMPLICATIONS

Some of the findings in this study suggest some serious implications for policy makers, administrators and extension workers. Some such implications are as-

1. Women devoted on an average 9 hrs/day in domestic chores. In slack agriculture season, they looked after the children and prepared food for the family, but during peak season, they could not devote much time in these activities. Economic compulsions forced them to neglect the children and their food, etc. the consequence of neglecting children and their food, etc. is much more serious than the probable consequence on farm. This can be minimized if mechanization be introduced on the farms so that on peak season, efficiency on the farm be increased, and, in turn, the curtailment of time stipulated for children be avoided.

2. Although, the women were found to involve themselves so much in farming, they have no adequate knowledge of modern technology of crop cultivation. It is on account

of their less educated or having no education. Hence, serious attempts be made to get them aware about modern technology. The agricultural universities should gear-up technical programmes of teaching, research and extension to the needs of farm women.

3. The programmes of KVKs and KGKs be expanded and the training programmes for women be intensified to enhance their productivity, liberate them from drudgeries of farm and household activities and also improve their skills leading to employability.
4. Strategies should be evolved to disseminate technologies to farm women. The appropriate technologies be developed for reducing drudgeries on the farm as well as in the home. Policy should be framed for sound feed back mechanism based on systematic monitoring and evaluation of such dissemination.
5. Policy makers should give consideration to income-generating technologies meant for women only. It should be kept in the mind of policy makers at the time of policy framing that women not only get training but also easy credit.
6. The physical structure and strength of women should be given due consideration by agricultural engineers while developing machinaries/equipments for farm.
7. Communication channels should be geared up for making aware women of new developments in farm sector.

CHAPTER 7

Summary and Conclusion

In our society, where economic power rests with the men, convention decreed that women's place is in the home, and that her husband's words are the law. They share the duties and responsibilities of maintaining their families on more than equal term with their men-folks but because of low visibility of their contribution, they are not regarded as equal partners in development process in spite of legal and constitutional equality.

Women are the cultural victims in our society which provides superiority to men and institutionalises deprivation to women. Though, they play dual roles, but patriarchal family system forced them behind the four walls of the house. This limits their mental horizon and they are considered incompetents to make major decisions.

The prosperity and the growth of India depends on the status and development of its women as they constitute nearly half of its population. All over the nation, they work long hours in market and non-market economy, and more so in rural India. The type of work, which they do depends on the social class to which they belong. Among the high socio-economic status households, they do not do manual work. like-wise in rural areas, women belonging to high socio-economic status households do not work on farms. The landless in rural areas work both in the fields as well as in the house or compound of the employer. This is because they have to supplement income of households to eke out.

This draws our attention to the plight and drudgery of rural women. The study area of Western Uttar Pradesh is no exception to this. The major issues which the present investigation proposed to address itself, are the following :

1. The multiple role of women in agriculture, allied agricultural activities and household activities.
2. Decision-making in farm and household affairs.
3. Knowledge, interest and adoption of modern technologies.
4. The nature and extent of women's involvement in agricultural and non-agricultural activities.
5. Appropriate technology identification for enhancing crop production and reducing drudgery faced by women. Technology should be efficient and income raising.

Rural women's participation in agriculture is a multi-faceted area for research. It is difficult to have a clear understanding and appreciation of their values and contribution unless all three major facts are studied in depth individually. Since a proper estimation of rural women's work has serious implications for human resources planning and development, it is found desirable to test the tenability of the above aspects through empirical analysis of data with the following specific objectives :-

1. To study the agro-climatic and socio-economic features of the study area with special reference to agricultural characteristics, occupational structure of working population and adoption of rural development programmes.
2. To study the socio-economic profile of the sample households and examine the existing resource position of households under study.
3. To study the extent of knowledge, interest and adoption of modern agricultural and home technologies by farm women.
4. To examine the nature and degree of involvement of rural women of different socio-economic groups in

farming systems and homestead activities, especially in terms of – (a) operations, (b) time spent and (c) period of involvement.

5. To examine the nature and level of employment of women in agricultural and non-agricultural sectors in the study area.
6. To identify the appropriate farm technologies which would provide the maximum advantages to rural women in terms of (a) enhancement of production efficiency, (b) increasing income, (c) reducing drudgery, and (d) increasing community participation.
7. To identify the socio-economic problems and suggest suitable policy measures for improving the status of rural women workers.

RESEARCH METHODOLOGY

The study was conducted in the two Western districts – Rampur and Bulandshahr of the Uttar Pradesh State. The two districts have been selected purposively as they have higher cropping intensities. For selection of samples, a multi-stage sampling procedure has been adopted. At first stage, two blocks from each district have been selected randomly, at second stage, five villages from each block were selected randomly and, at third stage, ten households from each selected village have been selected randomly. The selection of household was made after categorizing according to landholdings. Thus, in all one hundred households from each district have been selected and one women respondent was selected from each elected households. The data were collected with the help of structured interview schedule. Twelve socio-personal variables and four economic variables were selected as independent variables for the study. The dependent variables selected for the study were knowledge level, interest and adoption of technologies, role and status of women in agriculture, animal husbandry and household activities, decision-making pattern, drudgery index for five practices each of farm and animal husbandry, efficiency of modern agricultural technologies. For drudgery index, respondent's perception of drudgery was assessed by method of paired comparisons. Data for drudgery index were collected from thirty women respondents who were commonly involved in wheat and paddy crop production. Appropriate statistical techniques were applied for analysis of obtained data. The major findings of which are summarised below:

SOCIO-ECONOMIC PROFILE

The age of the respondents varied between 20-65 years in both the districts. The average age in Rampur district was 37 years whereas, in Bulandshahr, it was 41 years. This shows that middle-aged women, generally, get involved in work, be it of household or of outside. The inter-relationship among age, caste and education variables shows that respondents belonging to OBC households were mostly educated in both the districts. Only 6 respondents were above secondary passed in Rampur districts. Of this, two were of OBC an d four of Upper castes in the age-group 36-50 years. Regarding inter-relationship among caste, income and education of respondents, it was found that 23.08 per cent OBC respondents of Rampur district 11.36 per cent OBC respondents of Bulandshahr district carrying less than Rs. 1800 annually were having education up top primary level. The main occupation of respondents of Rampur district was farming, 9 per cent respondents were engaged in caste occupation and 29 per cent in business as secondary occupation. In Bulandshahr district, 94 per cent respondents were having farming as main occupation and 6 per cent farming as secondary occupation. In Rampur district, 43 per cent households were having marginal landholding, 18 per cent small and 23 per cent large holding. In Bulandshahr, the distribution of households according to land holding was almost of similar pattern. Overall, 41 per cent households were having marginal land holdings and 18 per cent were landless. In both the districts, 12.19 per cent households were having tractors and 40.86 per cent households were having up to two draught animals.

KNOWLEDGE AND ADOPTION OF TECHNOLOGIES

Adoption of technologies depends upon knowledge and interest of respondent in technologies. Of the 61 per cent respondents participating in wheat cultivation in Rampur district, 65.57 per cent respondents have knowledge of fertilizers and manures, 63.93 per cent intercultural operations, 60.66 per cent sowing and 47.54 per cent plant protection measures. Similarly, in Bulandshahr district, 65.52, 63.79, 55.17 and 51.72 per cent respondents have knowledge of intercultural operations, sowing fertilizers and manures and improved varieties, respectively.

Regarding paddy crop, it was observed by analysing pooled data that 72.44 per cent respondents were having knowledge of transplantation technology; 67.72 per cent nursery raising and 56.69 per cent seedbed preparation technology. In sugarcane cultivation, 75.61 per cent respondents were having knowledge of intercultural operations.

It was also observed that knowledge level of respondents have no association with their educational status. Whatever knowledge respondents were having about modern farm technologies were gained through work experience.

In case of animal husbandry and household technologies, knowledge of animal husbandry technologies has no association with educational status of respondent whereas it has association in household technologies. It indicates that for good knowledge of modern appliances and gadgets of domestic use, one should have at least secondary level education. The reason is that some electronic appliances are so complicated that uneducated can not understand its application.

Analysis of interest shown in farm technologies reveals that respondents have the highest interest in fertilizers and manures application in wheat and paddy cultivation in both the districts whereas their highest interest was in improved varieties used in sugarcane cultivation. In animal husbandry technologies, respondents were most interested in milk product preparation technology and least interested in breeding technology. In household technologies, they were highly interested in grain storage technologies and less interested in washing and ironing of clothes. The pattern of interest shown by the respondents of two districts was found to be non-significant in case of farm, animal husbandry and household technologies.

The adoption of farm technologies shows that respondents have adopted between 7 to 15 practices of wheat cultivation in

Rampur and 7 to 14 practice in Bulandshahr district. This shows no significant difference in the adoption of technologies of wheat and paddy crops. It was observed that respondents have not adopted plant protection measures, though they were having knowledge of and interest in this technology. The range of adoption of sugarcane cultivation technologies by respondents was found more in Rampur district than that of Bulandshahr district. In animal husbandry, respondents have the highest adoption of feeding technology and the least adoption of breeding technology. Respondents of both the districts have the highest adoption of grain storage technology and the least adoption of washing of clothes technology. The adoption of modern household appliances was affected on account of their highly unawareness about these. Some have awareness of these, but could not have adopted due to shortage of raw materials.

ROLE AND STATUS OF WOMEN

In traditional village community, the women have been playing a distinctive accepted role in the crop production. It was observed that 62.13 per cent respondents of both the districts of low income households have dominated role in intercultural operations, 55.39 per cent in harvesting and 40.78 per cent in transplanting. It was also observed that there was negative non-significant relationship between role of women and household income in transplanting, irrigation and nursery bed raising whereas significant in intercultural operations.

In animal husbandry, 53.33 per cent respondents of high income group households have dominating role in milk products preparation. In other activities, they have, generally, supportive role. In household activities, respondents of lower income group households of both the districts have dominating roles in fetching water and house cleaning activities. The respondents of high income group households have high supportive roles in food preparation, home cleaning and child care activities. It was also observed that with the increase in household income, the respondents of high income group devoted more time in domestic chores.

DECISION-MAKING PATTERN

The analysis of the decision-making pattern revealed that farm activities were more or less a male domain. In some activities such as sowing, post-sowing, harvesting and post-harvesting, husbands consulted their wives but in pre-sowing activity, they were the key decision-makers in both the districts. In carrying farm produce from field, 41.88 per cent respondents were the key-decision-makers. In both the districts, the pattern of decision-making in all the activities was similar, as no significant Z-values were found.

Regarding animal husbandry tasks, respondents of both the districts were key decision-makers in preparation of milk products, preparation of cow dung cakes, marketing and milking of animals activities. In household activities, the respondents were key decision-makers in the activities of house cleaning, stitching and sewing and fetching water whereas they made joint decisions in the activities of fetching fuel, child care, grain processing and storage and health care of members of the family. The child rearing was done by women, but husbands were of the view that decisions regarding health and education of children be made jointly. No significant difference was observed between the decision-making pattern in both the districts.

INVOLVEMENT OF WOMEN IN FARM AND HOMESTEAD ACTIVITIES

It was observed that significant negative relationship was existing between respondents involvement in farm operations and their educational status, and household income. This shows that respondents having low educational status and belonging to low income group households have high involvement in farm operations. It was observed that respondents on an average got an employment of 115.40 days/annum/head in crop production on the sampled households. Of this, she got light employment in harvesting of the crops, followed by interculture and sowing/transplanting of crops. District-wise, on an average, woman got an employment of 114.25 days/year in Rampur and 116.54 days/year in Bulandshahr districts.

In homestead activities, animal husbandry and household activities were studied. Women employment in animal husbandry activities according to income group of households shows that their employment in these activities declined with the increase in the household income, which was the highest (77.33 days/year) in the lowest income group and the lowest (53.30 days/year) in the highest income group. The average employment of 70.15 days/year/head was observed in Rampur and 71.80 days/year/head in Bulandshahr districts.

In household activities, the rural women spent substantial time. On an average, they spent 34.58 per cent of their time in food preparation and 30.60 per cent in child care and personal work. They spent, on an average, 9.02 hours in domestic activities, 4.96 hours in agricultural and 0.32 hours in non-agricultural activities per day. Household income group-wise analysis revealed that with the increase in income of the household they spent more time in domestic chores (9.27 hrs) and the women belonging to higher income group households did not involve themselves in non-agricultural activities. Similar findings were observed in case of educational status of respondents.

EMPLOYMENT OF WOMEN IN AGRICULTURE AND NON-AGRICULTURAL SECTORS

It was observed that women got an employment of 198.50 days per annum per head in the study areas. Of this, employment from agriculture sector was 186.38 days and 12.20 days from non-agriculture sector. Break-up of agriculture sector shows that, in crop production, it was to the extent of 115.40 days and in allied activities it was 70.98 days. In non-agriculture sector, 10.96 days employment in non-agriculture wages and 1.24 days in miscellaneous work. Household income-wise, the highest employment was in the tune of 200.73 days per annum in agriculture in the lowest income group and 144.17 days in the highest income group. This shows that employment in agriculture sector is indirectly related with the household income. In case of educational status of respondents, indirect relationship was observed between employment in agriculture sector and educational status of respondents. In non-agriculture sector, women of the lowest and medium income group households have employment whereas women of higher income group households have employment whereas women of higher income group households did not involve in this sector. The study also revealed that, out of 300 days available work in a year, 198.58 days women were employed and 101.42 days they were unemployed. In both the districts, the employment situation was somewhat similar.

IDENTIFICATION OF APPROPRIATE FARM TECHNOLOGIES

For identification of appropriate farm technology, the four criteria have been studied. They are (I) production efficient, (ii) income increasing, (iii) drudgery reducing and (iv) increasing community participation.

Out of eight technologies of wheat, seven of paddy and six of sugarcane crop, women adjudged irrigation the most appropriate technology for enhancing wheat production, use of transplanter for paddy and pre-sowing treatment for sugarcane production. In animal husbandry, they have adjudged breeding technology as production efficient.

The women adjudged use of improved varieties of wheat, paddy and sugarcane crops as the most income increasing technology. Regarding drudgery involved in operations, women have assigned the highest drudgery in transplanting of paddy and carrying fodder from field in animal husbandry activities. The use of transplanter for paddy crop and, for carrying fodder, small hand driven wheel cart would reduce their drudgery.

SOCIO-ECONOMIC PROBLEMS

The following socio-economic problems of women of study area were identified:-

1. Excess work load which is becoming less and less productive.
2. Non-recognition as a decision-maker.
3. Psychologically depressing environment.
4. Dependency on male members of the family.

5. Illiteracy resulting in lack of skills in conducting farming, family and social jobs.
6. Being traditionalist, women did not think to accept new occupational avenues.

Suggestions

To mitigate the sufferings of women, the following suggestions are being made:

1. Work simplification methods should be evolved by the agricultural scientists and be introduced with simple mechanical aids so that work load of women be lessened.
2. Women should be made aware of new farm technologies.
3. The infrastructure for dissemination of improved technologies and their use bc given in a package of know-how, raw materials and supporting aids.
4. The technologies should be indigenous and easily available to women.
6. The technologies should be drudgery reducing.
7. Appropriate technology should be introduced which may solve the fuel problem.
8. The women should be made aware of new agricultural tools and implements.
9. Demonstration and training camps should be organised fortnightly in every village for women only.
10. All efforts should be made to increase the active participation of women in technology generation, wherever required.

Policy implications

1. Mechanization be introduced in the farm to minimize the over burden of work of farm women.
2. Agriculture Universities should gear-up technical programmes of teaching, research and extension to get aware women about modern technologies.

3. KVKs and KGKs expand training programmes meant for women so that their productivity and skill be raised.
4. Appropriate technologies be developed for farm women so that their drudgery be reduced.
5. While framing policy, the policy makers should give consideration to income generating technologies for women. Women not only get training but also easy credit.
6. In developing of farm machinaries, physical structure and strength of women should be considered by agricultural engineers.
7. To get aware of new developments in farm sector, communication channels be geared up.

CONCLUSION

On the basis of the study, the following conclusions are drawn:-

1. More than half of the total respondents belonged to lower income group households. In Rampur district, 43 per cent households were having marginal land holdings and in Bulandshahr district, it was 39 per cent.
2. About 65.50 per cent respondents were between the age group 36.50 years and 46 per cent were educated up to primary level.
3. Knowledge level of the respondents have no association with their educational status regarding farm and animal husbandry technologies whereas significant association was found in case of household technologies.
4. The respondents were highly interested in fertilizers and manures application in wheat and paddy crops whereas improved varieties application in sugarcane crop. The pattern of interest shown by the respondents were almost similar in both the districts in case of farm, animal husbandry and household technologies.
5. In wheat cultivation, 42.02 per cent of total respondents have adopted all the practices of fertilizers and manures

application. In paddy, 31.50 per cent have full adoption of transplanting technology and, in sugarcane, 24.39 per cent have full adoption of irrigation and fertilizers and manures application. The range of adoption of practices of sugarcane cultivation in Rampur district was more than that of Bulandshahr district.

6. Respondents have the highest adoption of feeding technology among the animal husbandry technologies.
7. Respondents have the highest adoption of modern grain storage technology among the household technologies. Unawareness about modern household technologies was the main factor affecting the adoption of technologies.
8. Role of women respondents in farm operation have been affected by household income. It was observed that with the increase in household income the role of women in sowing/trasnplanting, nursery bed raising and irrigation operation decreased.
9. Role of women respondents in animal husbandry operations have been affected by household income. Except preparation of milk products, in other operations indirect relationship was observed.
10. The respondents of high income group families have supportive roles in food preparation, house cleaning and child care activities.
11. The decision-making pattern regarding farm activities in both the districts was found similar. In carrying farm produce from field, respondents were the key decision-makers whereas in case of harvesting, joint decisions were made by majority of the respondents. It was also observed that in 53.12 per cent low educational status households, decisions regarding money matters were taken jointly.
12. In animal husbandry tasks, high majority of respondents were the key decision-makers in preparation of milk products.

13. In household activities, large number of respondents were the key decision-makers in stitching and sewing of clothes and house cleaning. In child care activity, the decisions was taken jointly.

14. Respondents were employed for 115.40 days per annum per head in crop production and 70.98 days in animal husbandry tasks. Employment of respondents in crop production and animal husbandry task was indirectly related with their educational status and household income.

15. Time-utilization pattern of agricultural and non-agricultural activities in relation to household income and educational status of respondents reveals indirect relationship, whereas in case of household activities, it was directly related.

16. The average employment of respondents in agricultural and non-agricultural sectors was 186.38 and 12.20 days per annum per head, respectively.

17. Respondents identified irrigation application in wheat, transplanter use in paddy and pre-sowing of treatment in sugarcane as the most production efficient technologies. Improved varieties of wheat, paddy and sugarcane crops were identified as the most income increasing technologies. In animal husbandry, respondents adjudged breeding as the most production efficient technology. Regarding income increasing technology, preparation of milk products was adjudged the most income increasing technology by the respondents. .

18. Respondents have assigned the most drudgery involving technology to transplanting of paddy crops in crop production and carrying fodder from field in animal husbandry.

19. No effect of modern agricultural technologies on increase of community participation was observed.

Bibliography

Acharya, S. (1979). Transfer of Technology and Women Employment in India. Mimeograph, ICSSR, New Delhi.

Acharya, Sarthi (1986). *Women's Work and Economic Development – Women's Studies in India. Some Perspectives*. Ed. Maithregi Krishnaraj, Bombay: Popular Prakashan.

Agarwal, Hema (1987). A study on contribution of farm women in animal husbandry enterprise. An unpublished M.Sc. thesis submitted to IVRI, Izatnagar.

Agarwal, Vimla (1994). Stress and Multiple Role of Women. *The Indian Jr. of Soc. Sci*, 7(3&4): 319. Sage Publications, New Delhi.

Anandalakshmy, S. and G. Kelkar (1980). *Role of Women in Post-harvest Food Conservation*. United Nations University, Tokyo.

Anandalakshmy, S. and H.K. Sawhney (1988). Women's contribution to the productive processes in agriculture and the impact of modernization. Abstract, Int. Conf. On Appropriate Agric. Tech. for Farm Women, ICAR, New Delhi, Nov.-Dec.

Arya, B.S. (1964). Role of family in Decision-making on Related to Farm Operation. An unpublished M. Sc. Thesis, Division of Agricultural Extension, IARI, New Delhi.

Badran, H. (1972). Arab Women in National Development. A study of three Arab countries – prepared for the seminar on Arab Women in National Development, Cairo. Sponsored by UNICEF in Co-operation with the League of Arab States Functional Literacy Centre.

Bajwa, Gurdeep K. (1983). A comparative study of role performance if women from farm owning and non-farm owing families in selected agricultural operations. An unpublished M.Sc. thesis submitted to Punjab Agricultural University, Ludhiana.

Bakashi, R.M. (1970). A study of the impact of Govt. Milk Supply Scheme, Jabalpur on the Dairy farmers around Jabalpur city. An unpublished M.Sc. thesis, JNKV, Jabalpur.

Bala, N. and S. Roy (1979). Utilization of household knowledge of farm women. *Ind. J. Edu.*, 15(3&4) : 22-26.

Baskara Rao, N. (1995). Irrigated agriculture and female work participation. *The Ind. Jr. of Social Sci.*, 8(2): 171-84. Sage Publications, New Delhi.

Behari, Bepin (1991). Rural Technological Adaptation. Rural Poverty, Unemployment Technology and Rural Poverty Book.

Bhati, J.P. and D.V. Singh (1987). Women's contribution to agricultural economy in hill regions of North-west India. *Eco. and Pol. Weekly*, 22(17): 7-11.

Bhatia, V. and R. Deshpandey (1972). A study of acceptors discontinuous and non-acceptors of smokeless chullah in one village of Delhi. published in "Studies of the Rural Community" compiled by Renu Chahil, Lady Irwin College, New Delhi, pp. 31-34.

Bhatti, Z. (1987). *Economic contribution of women to the household budget: A case study of the beedi industry.* Invisible Hands: Women in Home-based production. Sage Publications, New Delhi.

Boserup, E. (1970). *Women Role in Economic Development.* George Allen and Unwin, New York.

Chakraborty, S.P. (1990). *Role of agri-tools and equipments in Indian farming.* National Metallurgical Laboratory, Jamshedpur, pp. 71-79.

Charulata (1997). Drudgery correlates of men and women involved in paddy cultivation. *Ind. Jr. of Extn. Edu.*, 33(1&2).

Chattopadhyay, R.N. (1998). Transfer of Technology for Rural Development: A stride towards livelihood generation in the rural sectors. Jr. of Rural Dev., 17(3): 537-39.

Chaudharı, Chayanika (1973). A study on the participation and interest of rural school-going adolescent farm girls in food production and home management. Review of Research Studies on Women in Agriculture in India, ICAR, New Delhi, pp. 61.

Chopra, R. (1980). Impact of television on gain and retention of knowledge among farmers. Research on Farm Radio and Television Programmes, compiled by B.S. Hansara and A.N. Shukla, PAU, Ludhiana.

Dahiya, A. and M. Gupta (1993). Role expectations of working couples regarding household work. Maharashtra Jr. of Extn. Edu., 20 : 205-8.

Dak, T.M.; M.L. Sharma and R. Jain (1986). Role of women in agriculture-an investigation into socio-economic correlates affecting changes in their work participation. Abstract, Seminar on Role of Development Programmes on Socio-economic Status of Women. Haryana Agricultural University, Hisar, March, 21-22.

Das, S.K. G. Padhi and M. Jena (1996). Role of women in rice cultivation and technology adoption. *Indian Farming*: 35-37, Dec.

Deepali, M.N. (1979). A study on the knowledge and participation of rural women in agricultural operations with respect of paddy crop and their value orientation in Dharwad district. Review of Research Studies on Women in Agriculture in India. ICAR, New Delhi, pp. 60.

Devadas, Rajammal, P.(1999). Appropriate home science technologies for promoting status of the women. C. Prasad and T. Balaguru edited book Women In Agriculture – Development Issues. Proceedings of the National Seminar, Dec. 28-30, 1993, pp. 269-76.

Dhawan, K.C. and S.S. Zohal (1967). Comparative profitability of diary enterprises in relation to cultivation on sub-urban farm in Punjab. *Ind. Jr. Agril. Econ.*, 22: 81-97.

Dhesai, J.K.; S.Shahid, and D.M. Engira (1981). Investigation of the performance of a reflector type solar cooker for an Indian Kitchen. *Indian Jr. Home Science*, 14(1): 13-16.

Dixon, R.B. (1993). *Employment for Rural Women Five Programmes. Rural women at work.* Strategies for Development in South Asia. Baltimore and London.

Dixon, R.B. (1982). Women in Agriculture: Counting the Labour Force in Developing Countries. *Population and Development Review*, 8(3): 5339-56.

Dubey, V.K. (1988). All work and no play. *Indian Farming*, 38 (8) : 7.

Duggal, Binoo (1985). A study on fuel utilization and user need fulfillment of smokeless chullah in selected Haryana village. An unpublished M.Sc. thesis, Haryana Agricultural University, Hisar.

Edwards, A.C. (1969). *Techniques of Attitude Scale Construction.* Vakil, Felfer and Simons Pvt. Ltd., Mumbai.

Ethelebert, J.M. (2000). Status of women for present and future generation. Abstract. *Proceedings of Int. Women's Conf. On Women's Status : Vision & Reality*, New Delhi, Feb.-March, p. 185.

Executive Summary (2002) *Tenth Plan: Animal Husbandry and Dairying*. A Report of Tenth Five-year Plan (2002-07), Planning Commission, Govt. of India, January.

Gandhi, S.; Lali Yadav and Sarita Singhal (1986). Women's role and contribution in home and farm sectors. Abstract, Seminar on Role of Development Programmes on Socio-economic Status of Women, Haryana Agricultural University, Hisar, March 21-22.

Ghosh, S. (2001). Constraints in adoption of recommended technologies for improved dairy farming. *Ind. Jr. of Extn. Edu.*, 37(1&2) : 24.

Ghosh, S. and M.M. Adhikary (1988). Role of village women in decision-making in different farm economic business. Abstract, *Int. Conf. On Appro. Agric. Tech. for Farm Women*, ICAR, Nov.-Dec., p. 26.

Godara, R. (1997). Knowledge level and technological gap in cotton cultivation. An unpublished M. Sc. thesis submitted to Haryana Agricultural University, Hisar.

Grover, I. and D.K. Grover (1993). Farm women face wage and job discriminations in North-Western India. *Indian Farming*, June, 1993.

Gupta, V.S. (2001). Literacy and technology for rural development. Mutual relationship. *Kurukshetra*, Annual Issue: 25-29, Oct.

Gurusamy, S. (1987). Role of women in decision-making process of dryland farming. An unpublished M. Sc. (Ag.) dissertation submitted to the Tamil Nadu Agricultural University, Coimbatore.

Hira Nand; J.P. Sharma and Janardanjee (1988). Contribution of ram women to farm operations and decision-making there on with special reference to potato. Central Potato Research Institute, Simla.

Indravati, V. Sangwan and S. Gandhi (1992). Drudgery reduction of rural women in household activities in action research. Int. Jr. of Social Res., 33(3): 222-29.

Jain, D. (1980). Milk Producers of Kaira Women's Quest for Power. Vikas Publishing House, New Delhi.

Jain, T. and K. Khanna (1971). A study on the process of diffusion of information through key women to the caste groups. Published in Studies of the Rural Community, Compiled by Renu Chahil, Lady Irwin College, New Delhi, 1972, pp. 192-194.

Jain, Veena (1981). A study on improved home practices as perceived by farm women, an unpublished M. Sc. thesis submitted to Haryana Agricultural University, Hisar.

Jain, Vinita (1991). Inter-gender drudgery in animal husbandry operations among rural families. An unpublished M. Sc. thesis submitted to Haryana Agricultural University, Hisar.

Jamal, S. and K. Singh (1984). Suitability of nutrition and home management practices and communication behaviour among farm women. An unpublished M. Sc. thesis submitted to G.B. Pant Univ. of Agril. & Tech., Pantnagar.

Jamal, Shagufta (1989). A study of role dynamics of farm women in relation to productivity of dairy animals. An unpublished Ph.D. thesis submitted to IVRI, Izatnagar.

Jayanthi, P. (1995). Profile of women entrepreneurs in Pollachi taluk, Coimbatore district. An unpublished M. Sc. thesis submitted to Avinashlingam Deemed University, Coimbatore.

Jesani, A. (1990). Limits of empowerment women in rural health care. *Eco. and Pol. Weekly*, 25(5-12): 1098-1103.

Jhansi Rani, G. (1981). Decision-making pattern among rural families and type of participation by rural women in selected areas of decisions. An unpublished M. Sc. thesis submitted to Andhra Pradesh Agricultural University, Hyderabad.

Jones, R.L. and S.K. Jones (1976). *The Himalayan Women*, Mayfield, Palo Alto.

Joshy, Anil, P. and Kiran Rawat (2001). Choice of technologies for women. *Kurukshetra*, Annual Issue: 20-24, Oct.

Kalaimathi, A. (1988). Labour force participation of women in agriculture. *Journal of Ravishankar University*, 1(1): 123-135.

Kanwar, B.S. and J.S. Guleria (1988). Role of women in agriculture. Abstract, *Ind. Conf. On Appropriate Agric. Tech. for Farm Women*, ICAR, New Delhi, Nov.-Dec., p. 39.

Kashyap, S. (1988). Human resource development of rural women with special reference to time-wise analysis and feasibility of vocational trainings. An unpublished Ph.D. thesis submitted to Haryana Agricultural University, Hisar.

Kaur, Malkiat (1986). *Female work participation in rural Haryana. Impact of technological Advancements in Agriculture*. D.K. Publisher, New Delhi.

Kaur, Malkiat and M.C. Sharma (1991). *Technology and work patterns of rural women*. R.K. Punia edited book Women in Agriculture, Vol. 1: Their Status and Role, Northern Book Centre, New Delhi.

Kaur, Malkiat and M.L. Sharma (1988). In the heartland of Haryana Men Command Machines, driving women to drudgery work. *Indian Farming*: 11-16, Nov.

Kaur, R. and N. Mahajan (1993). Performance of agricultural related roles by farm women. *Agric. Extn. Review*, 5(1): 19-23.

Kaur, Satnam (1987). *Women in Rural Development. A Case Study. Book Review*, Mittal Publications, Delhi.

Kaur, Swaranjeet (1981). A comparative study of role performance of women from farm owning and non-farm owning families in selected agricultural operations. An unpublished M. Sc. thesis submitted to Punjab Agriculture University, Ludhiana.

Khandekar, N. and O.N. Kunzru (1997). Involvement of tribal women in decision-making in Madhya Pradesh, *Maharastra Jr. of Extn. Edu.*, 8(3) : 1730-34.

Kishwar, M. (1996). It it's Sunday, it must be her holiday, *Sunday Times*, Aug. 18.

Krishnamurthy, K. and K.R. Kulkarni (1988). Appropriate agricultural technology for farm women. Abstract. Int. Conf. On Appropriate Agri.-Tech. for Farm Women, ICAR, New Delhi, Nov.-Dec., p.13.

Kulkarni, S.Y.; M.R. Alshi and Kalpana V. Kakde (1988). Role of farm women in agriculture with particular reference to magnitude of labour use and employment. Abstract. *Int. Conf. On Appropriate Agric.-Tech. for Farm Women*, ICAR, New Delhi, Nov-Dec., p. 17.

Kumar, Anil (1990). Development and popularization of efficient agricultural tools and implement for hill agriculture. Published in *Rural Development in India: Engineering Application*, ICAR, New Delhi, pp. 66-72.

Kunwar, N.; S.M. Dingar and J.P. Singh (1991-94). Participation pattern of rural women in home and farm activities. *Farm Sci. Jr.*, 6-9:96-101.

Kunwar, Neelama (1993). A study on the contribution of women in farm and home management with special reference to Rampur district of Uttar Pradesh. Unpublished Ph. D. thesis, B.R. Ambedkar University, Agra.

Kunwar, Neelam (1996). Evaluation of transfer of grain storage technology to rural women. *Jr. Dairying, Foods & Home Sci.*, 15(1): 64-68.

Kunzru, O.N. and Hema Tripathi (1999). Role of women in animal husbandry enterprises – A successful experience. C. Prasad and T. Balaguru edited *Women in Agriculture – Developmental Issues*. Proceedings of the National Seminar, Dec. 28-30, 1993, pp. 254-62.

Lal, J.N. (1987). *Status of rural women in Eastern U.P. Project Report*, ICSSR, New Delhi.

Laxmi Devi, A. (1987). *Rural Women: Management in Farm and Home*. Northern Book Centre, New Delhi.

Laxmi Devi, A. (1991). Farm role of women in Andhra Pradesh,. R. K. Punia edited book *Women in Agriculture*, Vol. 1: Their Status and Role, Northern Book Centre, New Delhi.

Lepcha, Tseten Tashi (1987). A study of farm women's contribution to agricultural production in eastern district of Sikkim state. An unpublished M.Sc. thesis, Gujarat Agricultural University, Anand.

Mahajan, Neelam and Y.P. Singh (1982). Transfer of home making practices. Ind. Jr. Home Sci., 14: 11-17.

Malik, J.S.; Rajendra Kumar and Manju Singh (1999). Role of Indian women in different aspects of daily life. *Intensive Agric*. Pp. 22-23, March-April.

Manick, TS. And G. Manimegali (1988). Appropriate home science technologies for the upliftment of rural women. Abstract, Int. Conf. On Appropriate Agric. Tech. for Farm Women, ICAR, New Delhi, Nov.-Dec., p. 169.

Maratha, A.C. (1988). Women's work in Indian agricultural by agro-ecological zones-Meeting needs of landless and poor. *Eco. and Pol. Weekly*, 24: 79-85.

Maurya, Ram Deen (1986). *Women in India : A Demographic Profile*, pp. 94-116.

Mazumdar, S. (1983). Women participation in agricultural and non-agricultural activities in Bangladesh villages. GTU Publication: Bangladesh Agricultural University (Bangladesh) No. 39, p.18.

Mc Auley, Alastair (1985). Women's Involvement in Agriculture, 1960-75. *Women Work and Wages in the Soviet Union*, George Allen & Unwin, Boston, Sydney.

Muniratnam, G. and A.B. Srilatha (1999). Adoption and diffusion of dairy farming practices for farm women in Chittoor district. A case study, C. Prasad and T. Balaguru edited *Women in Agriculture - Developmental Issues*. Proceedings of the National Seminar, Dec. 28-30, 1993 pp. 135-42.

Naghrahman, D. and S. Sambrani (1983). Women drudgery in fire wood collection. *Eco. and Pol. Weekly*, 18(1/2): 35-38.

Nataraju, M.S. and P.G. Lovely (1989). Role of farm women in farm and home activities. *Interaction*, 50: 64-67.

Nath, K. (1968). Women in the working force in India. *Eco. and Pol. Weekly*, 31: 1205-15.

Niranjan, Man Singh (1976). Role of farm women in agricultural production and home making. An unpublished M.Sc. (Ag.) thesis submitted to C.S. Azad Univ. Of Agric. And Tech., Kanpur.

Pandey, U.K.; H.S. Malik; K.S. Suhag and L. Rai (1988) Participation of rural women in Haryana agriculture. *Agril. Situation in India*, 42(11); 969-74.

Panhwar, F. (2003). Women and organic agriculture in Pakistan. http;//www. Pakistan. Com/English/advisory/ organic. Farming/women and organic. Shtml.

Parthawarathy, G. (1996). Recent trends in wages and employment agricultural labour. *Ind. Jr. of Agri. Econ.*, 51(1,2): 145-67.

Pauililo, M.I.S. (1976). The work of women in rural areas. World Agricultural Economics and Rural Sociology. Abstracts, 20(9): 645.

Pavghal, B.S,. and Mange Ram (1985). Employment pattern of women labour in Haryana agriculture (summary). *Ind. Jr, Agric. Econ.*, 40(3) : 273.

Pradhan, Meena (1990). Women in Agriculture. *Indian Farmer Times*, New Delhi, Nov. pp. 19-20.

Punia, R.K. (1980). Changing Agrarian Structure in Haryana. An unpublished Ph. D. thesis submitted to Haryana Agricultural University, Hisar.

Punia, R.K.; Satnam Kaur and Deep Punia (1991). Women in agricultural production process in Haryana. R.K. Puinia edited book *Women In Agriculture*. Vol. 1: Their Status and Role Northern Book Centre, New Delhi.

Puri, S. (1972). *Work role and decision-making pattern of farm wives and husbands*. An unpublished Ph.D. thesis submitted to Division of Agricultural Extension, IARI, New Delhi.

Rajmal P. Devdas, Pankajan Sundram and S. Sithalakshmi (1988). Appropriate home science technologies with their implications to farm women and farming, abstract, *Int. Conf. Ion Appropriate Agric. Tech. for Farm Women*, ICAR New Delhi. Nov.-Dec., p. 165.

Rajmal, P.D.; H. Pandey and Muthian (1991). Socio-economic study of farm women in rainfed agriculture and the rile of Krishi Vigyan Kendra. Abstract, *Int. Conf. In Extension Strategy for Minimizing Risk in Rainfed Agriculture*, New Delhi.

Rajvanshi, J. (1990). Economic independence of educated working and non-working women. *Ind.. Jr. of Social Res.*, 31: 100-06.

Ramsey, C.E., R.A. Polson and G. Splencer (1959). Values and addition of practices. *Rural Sociology*, 24(1) : 35-47.

Roggers, E.M. (1962). *Diffusion of Innovations*. The Free Press, New York.

Ruth, Nilaklantha (1980). *Measuring rural unemployment in India – A methodological note* (unpublished paper) Gokhale Institute of Politics and Economics, Pune.

Saikia, P. (1983). Seasonal variation of female participation farm work. *Kurukshetra*, 31(19) : 15-17.

Saini, Harmindar (1983). Time take analysis of farming and non-farming home maker. *Review of Research Studies on Women in Agriculture in India*. Published by ICAR, New Delhi.

Sampath, R.KJ. (1979). Nature and measurement of economic efficiency in Indian Agriculture. *Ind. Jr. Agril. Econ.*, 34: 17-34.

Sankaran, S. And Rani Perumal (1999). Tamil Nadu agriculture and farm women. C. Prasad and T. Balaguru edited *Women in Agriculture - Developmental Issues*. Proceedings of the National Seminar, Dec. 28-30, 1993 pp. 85-96.

Sardana, P.K.; Sudesh Gandhi; R.C. Hasija and S.D. Chamola (1988). Role of women in agriculture: Farm women and dairy cattle supplement one another. *Jr. of Extn. System*, 4(1): 67-69.

Satapathy, C. (1987). Women in agriculture: A study at adopted villages of OUAT Research Project Report, Orissa University of Agriculture and Technology, Bhubaneshwar.

Savitri and Geeta (1990). Indira Gandhi – the Greatest Women of the 20th Century. Book : Women in India: Indian Women, Publication Division, Ministry of Information and 'Broadcasting, Govt. of India, New Delhi. pp. 81-95.

Saxena, Daya and Suman Rani Bhatnagar (1985). A comparative study of time utilization pattern of tribal and non-tribal women in Rajasthan. *Ind. Jr. Extn.*, 21: 83-85.

Sen, D. (1993). Role transition of women in agriculture: Some issues. *Jr. of Rural Dev.*, 12(5): 497-513.

Sethi, Raj Mohini (1990). *Work participation of women house-work*. Published in Book Women in Agriculture. Rawat Publications, Jaipur, New Delhi. pp. 78-85.

Shanmugasundaram, Yasodha (1993). Women Employment in India: With Special Reference to Tamil Nadu. Book Published Institute of Advanced Studies Research, Madras.

Sharma, D.K. and T.R. Singh (1970). Participation of women in decisions related to farm business. *Ind. Jr. Ext. Edu.*, 6(1-2): 43-49.

Sharma , Promila and Nalaini Ogale (2000). Decision-making profile of women farmers in management of farm households of hill region of Uttar Pradesh. Abstract. *Proceedings of Int. Women's Conf. On Women's Status: Vision & Reality*, New Delhi, Feb.-March, p. 234.

Shatrunga, V. (1990). Experiencing drudgery. *Eco. and Pol. Weekly*, 25(16): 292-235.

Singh, B. (1983). Participation of tribal women in farm business in relation to their socio-economic characteristics: A selected analysis" *Institute Social Res. Jr.,* 3: 24-31.

Singh, H. (1967). Resource re-allocation and enterprises combination – A case study of U.P., *Agricultural Situation in India*, 22(9) : 987-96.

Singh, J.R. (1968). Participation of rural women in decision-making process related to farm business with special reference to farm families in NES block. An unpublished M. Sc. thesis submitted to J.N. Krishi Vishwavidayalay of College of Agriculture, Jabalpur.

Singh, J.N. (1982). A study of the suitability of dairy farming innovations and factors associated with their adoption by cattle owners of Intensive Cattle Development Project, Gurgaon (Haryana). An unpublished Ph. D. thesis submitted to Kurukshetra University, Kurukshetra.

Singh, M.P. and Neeraj Sharma (1991). Women in rice based farming system in Uttar Pradesh. R.K. Punia edited book *Women in Agriculture*, Vol., 1: Their Status and Role, Northern Book Centre, New Delhi pp. 97-109.

Sinha, M. (1983). Educational Achievement. *Review of Educational Research*, 25: 15.

Sinha, S.P. (1980). Impact of technological development in agriculture on women in rural areas. A two village profile (Muzaffarpur, North Bihar). An unpublished Project Report sponsored by ICSSR, New Delhi.

Sreedevi, K. (1984). Time management of rural women in home and farm activities. Review of Research Studies on Women in Agriculture in India. Published by ICAR, New Delhi, pp. 63.

Srivastava, J.C. (1985). Harnessing technology for improving the quality of life in rural women. In: *Women and Technology*, Jain , S.C. (ed.) Rawat Publications, Jaipur, pp. 38-74.

Subrahamanyam, K.V. (1975). Adoption of new technology in small farm: The role of credit and its requirements, *Ind. Jr. Agril. Econ.*, 30: 181-85.

Sudharani, P. and V.T. Raju (1991). Participation of women in agricultural operations. *Ind. Jr. of Extn. Edu.*, 27(1&2).

Thakur, Sonia (1997). Inter-gender drudgery in agricultural and livestock operations of West zone of Haryana. Unpublished Ph.D. thesis, CCS Haryana Agricultural University, Hisar.

Tinker, I. (1980). *Women and Energy Programme Implication*. pp. 11.

Tripathi, H. and H.P.S. Arya (1988). Time utilization pattern of farm women in animal husbandry enterprise. Abstract: Int. Conf. On Appropriate Agri.-Tech. for Farm Women, ICAR, New Delhi., Nov.-Dec.

Tripathi, Hema (!991). Productivity of milch animals and employment generation for rural women. An unpublished M. Sc. thesis submitted to IVRI, Izatnagar.

Tripathi, S.N., and Saudamini Das (1990). *Informal Women Labour in India*. Discovery Publishing House, New Delhi.

Trivedi, G. (1963). Measurement and analysis of socio-economic status of rural families. An unpublished Ph.D. thesis submitted to Div. of Agril. Extn., IARI, New Delhi.

Usha, S.S. Miglani and A.J. Singh (1983). Female labour participation in Fardikot district (Punjab State). *J. Res. Punjab Agric. Univ.*, 29(4): 525-35.

Varma, S.K. (1989). Farm women in the changing agro-economic scenario. An unpublished Ph. D. thesis submitted to IARI, New Delhi.

Index